PENNSYLVANIA SNACKS

PENNSYLVANIA SNACKS

A Guide to
Food Factory Tours

Sharon Hernes Silverman

STACKPOLE
BOOKS

Published by
STACKPOLE BOOKS
5067 Ritter Road
Mechanicsburg, PA 17055
www.stackpolebooks.com

Printed in the United States of America

10 9 8 7 6 5 4 3 2 1

FIRST EDITION

COVER DESIGN BY WENDY REYNOLDS
FRONT COVER PHOTO COURTESY OF HERR FOODS
BACK COVER PHOTO COURTESY OF PHILADELPHIA CANDIES
INTERIOR PHOTOS BY SHARON HERNES SILVERMAN, UNLESS OTHERWISE NOTED
LOGOS USED WITH PERMISSION OF THE MANUFACTURERS

Library of Congress Cataloging-in-Publication Data

Silverman, Sharon Hernes.
    Pennsylvania snacks : a guide to food factory tours / Sharon Hernes
Silverman.—1st ed.
        p.   cm.
    Includes index.
    ISBN 0-8117-2874-9
    1. Food processing plants—Pennsylvania—Guidebooks.

TP373 .S43   2001
664'.6—dc21
                                                                00-053834

Contents

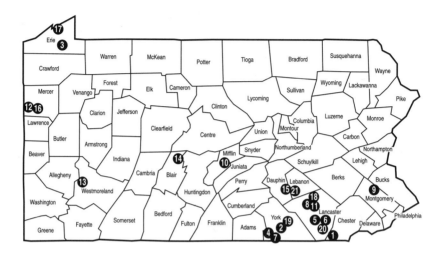

Potato Chips

1 Herr Foods, *Nottingham*

2 Martin's Potato Chips, *Thomasville*

3 Troyer Potato Products, *Waterford*

4 Utz Quality Foods, *Hanover*

Pretzels

5 Anderson Bakery Company, *Lancaster*

6 Intercourse Pretzel Factory, *Intercourse*

7 Snyder's of Hanover, *Hanover*

8 Sturgis Pretzel House, *Lititz*

Chocolate and Candy

9 Asher's Chocolates, *Souderton*

10 Asher's/Lewistown, *Lewistown*

Chocolate and Candy *(continued)*

11 Cake And Kandy Emporium, *Lititz*

12 Daffin's Candies, *Sharon*

13 Sherm Edwards Candies, *Trafford*

14 Gardners Candies, *Tyrone*

15 Hershey's Chocolate World, *Hershey*

16 Philadelphia Candies, *Hermitage*

17 Pulakos 926 Chocolates, *Erie*

18 Wilbur Chocolate Candy Americana Museum
& Store, *Lititz*

19 Wolfgang Candy Company, *York*

Regional Specialties

20 Intercourse Canning Company, *Intercourse*

21 Seltzer's Smokehouse Meats, *Palmyra*

Introduction

S nacking is alive and well in Pennsylvania, and so is the snack food industry. The Keystone State is the birthplace of commercial pretzel baking in the country, the United States' leading manufacturer of potato chips, and the nation's top candy producer, excluding gum.

With the pace of snack food sales on the increase—up 6.2 percent in 1999, according to the Snack Food Association (SFA)—the state's snack industry is likely to continue enjoying its successful run. Using potato chips as a barometer, one sees steady growth. In 1999, sales of potato chips reached $4.69 billion in this country. That's a lot of chips.

Pennsylvania is fortunate to have several categories of snack-making factories that offer tours: chips, pretzels, chocolate and candy, and regional specialties.

I began my search for Pennsylvania snack companies that give tours by poring over guidebooks, directories, brochures, magazines, and websites. I also contacted convention and visitors bureaus, tourist promotion agencies, chambers of commerce, and trade organizations to find likely candidates to include in this book.

Once I had a list of manufacturers, I got in touch with each one to inquire about tours. Some companies had never given tours; others had discontinued their tours due to insurance regulations, liability concerns, or the need to use the space in a different way. (Benzel's Pretzels in Altoona, which many people ask me about, falls into the last category.) I sent a detailed questionnaire to each of the remaining companies.

Then I hit the road.

I personally took the tour at every company listed in this book, in order to be able to give you a firsthand description of what you can expect to see when you visit. Different styles of tours will appeal to different people; you may prefer tours that go right down on the factory floor, whereas if you have small children, you might opt for a tour that looks through gallery windows and doesn't get so close to heavy machinery. This book gives you all the information you need to choose the kind of tour that's best for you.

POTATO CHIPS

We Americans sure do love potato chips. Each year, Americans consume $4.5 billion worth of the snack, according to the Snack Food Association (SFA), the international trade association of the snack food industry. That's more than any other people in the world.

So how did the potato chip come to be? Believe it or not, the country's favorite snack food was not a result of culinary genius, but a fit of pique.

Thomas Jefferson is credited with bringing the recipe for french fried potatoes back from France in the late 1700s. This thick-cut potato dish quickly became popular. By the mid-nineteenth century, fried potatoes often appeared on restaurant menus.

One such menu was at Moon Lake Lodge in tony Saratoga Springs, New York, the top summer getaway for the rich and famous of the time. With its proximity to New York City, it drew high-society folks who were looking for a cool country vacation.

In the summer of 1853, George Crum was the chef at Moon Lake Lodge. Various accounts describe Crum's heritage as American Indian, African American, or both, but they are universal in describing him as an irascible character.

A patron placed an order for french fries; when the order arrived, he found the potatoes sliced too thick for his liking, so he sent them back. Chef Crum cut and fried thinner potatoes, but the exacting diner rejected these too. Back to the kitchen they went.

One can imagine Crum's attitude when the potatoes were returned a second time. "He wants thin? I'll give him thin!" the chef might have muttered. He proceeded to cut the potatoes so thin and to fry them so crisply that they would be impossible to eat with a fork.

Crum might have been rubbing his hands together in glee as he peeked from the kitchen to see the patron's reaction to what the chef

Opposite: Potato chips drop into scales at Herr Foods. COURTESY OF HERR FOODS INC.

Potato Particulars

It's been quite a journey for the potato, from its origins in South America to the snack factories of Pennsylvania.

The potato was discovered and cultivated in the Andes Mountains by pre-Columbian farmers several thousand years ago. Spanish conquistadors were the first Europeans to become acquainted with the tuber, but the Spanish did not give it a position of prominence. In Spain's colonies, potatoes were thought of as food for the lower classes. Back home, they were fed to hospital patients.

Despite its nutritional richness, the potato was accepted slowly in Europe, for a variety of reasons. One was its membership in the nightshade family. This botanical classification also includes poisonous plants, such as belladonna, or deadly nightshade. The leaves of the potato are, in fact, poisonous.

At last, the potato began to gain favor in Europe and was brought to North America as well. In Colonial times, New Englanders primarily used potatoes to feed pigs. They didn't think that people should eat potatoes, not because of nutritional concerns, but because they ascribed aphrodisiac properties to it. They feared that the behavior engendered by such a substance could lead to exhaustion—and a shorter life.

In the 1840s, the European crop was decimated by blight. North American potatoes escaped the terrible disease, and potatoes went on

thought was an inedible dish. Instead of being displeased with the paper-thin potatoes, the guest was delighted, and a new craze was born. Other diners at Moon Lake Lodge began requesting the "potato crunches," which soon appeared on the menu as Saratoga Chips, a specialty of the house.

The patron whose fussiness led Crum to invent the potato chip is sometimes identified as Cornelius Vanderbilt, but this may be name-dropping more than fact. True, Vanderbilt was at Saratoga and probably dined at the restaurant, but there is no proof that he was the one who sent back the potatoes. He did, however, join several others in supplying financial backing so that George Crum could open his own restaurant at to become a major food crop. Worldwide, potatoes are second in human consumption only to rice. Varieties were developed for different purposes, including baking and chipping.

The Keystone State is the premier state when it comes to chipping potatoes. With 20,000 acres of potatoes, it ranks thirteenth in the nation in potato production. It takes about 4 pounds of potatoes to make a pound of potato chips.

The chipping potatoes used by Pennsylvania snack manufacturers are chosen for low moisture content, round shape, and resistance to bruising. They are also lower in sugar than their baking potato counterparts. Agriculturists and manufacturers are working together to improve the storage properties and chipping suitability of potatoes.

The Plano, Texas, based Frito-Lay Company has had a strong Pennsylvania presence since it purchased a York facility from Eagle Snacks, Inc., in 1996, but despite the arrival of this snack food giant and the continuing consolidation as small companies are engulfed by larger ones, Pennsylvania sustains a substantial number of local and regional manufacturers. Currently, Snyder of Berlin, which offers no public tours, is the largest user of Pennsylvania-grown potatoes in the industry. A faithful local following, as well as easy access to Washington, Baltimore, Philadelphia, and New York, have helped the "little guys" survive and thrive, and the area around Hanover and York is even nicknamed the "Potato Chip Belt."

the south end of the lake. Crum put baskets of the crunches out on the tables, and they were a big draw. He also packed the chips in boxes and sold them as Saratoga Chips.

At that time, potatoes were peeled and sliced by hand, so chip making was highly labor-intensive. Between their 1853 invention and the early twentieth century, potato chips were primarily a restaurant item.

William Tappendon of Cleveland was one of the first entrepreneurs to make chips to sell in grocery stores, back in 1895. He was so successful that he moved his frying operation from his kitchen into a specially converted barn, a location that the Snack Food Association calls one of the nation's first potato chip factories.

Three 1920s inventions revolutionized the production and distribution of potato chips. First was the invention of the mechanical potato peeler. Next was the 1926 development of the waxed paper bag for chips, credited to Laura Scudder of Scudder's Potato Chip Factory in Monterey Park, California. Women employees took home sheets of waxed paper and ironed them into bags. The next day, the bags were filled with chips and the tops ironed shut so that the bags could be delivered to retailers. Prior to this, potato chips were sold from cracker barrels or glass display cases.

The third invention came in 1929, when the first continuous potato chip cooker was invented by Freeman McBeth of the J. D. Ferry Company. Until then, potato chips were kettle-cooked in small batches. The fryer, which offered huge economies of scale, was given to the Ross Potato Chip Company in Richland, Pennsylvania, and—after the torpor of the Depression—the potato chip industry was off and running, as other companies adopted the technology. By 1933, preprinted glassine bags made it possible for manufacturers to stamp their brands onto the bags. Potato chips had completed the transition from restaurant specialty item to snack food.

Pennsylvania is the nation's top chipping potato state. Thirteenth in overall potato output, 70 percent of the state's potato acreage is planted with chipping potatoes; this translates into $57 million worth of potato chips per year.

The Keystone State is also the most important producer of potato chips. Go into any supermarket or convenience store, and you'll see shelves and shelves of potato chips, not just from the big national brands, but also from the smaller regional companies. Strong brand loyalty, profitable regional markets, and the recession-proof nature of the snack food industry—when times are tough, people buy lots of snacks—have enabled smaller producers to remain profitable without being swallowed up by the larger manufacturers. You, however, can swallow up their products fresh from the factory. Crunch!

Herr Foods

Routes 1 and 272
20 Herr Drive
P.O. Box 300
Nottingham, PA 19362
800-63-SNACK
www.herrs.com

On one level, the Herr's story is about snack foods, business, and commercial success. On another level, the story is about family and faith, hard times and hard work, community and continuity. It's about people.

The company's founder, James S. Herr, grew up on his Mennonite family's Lancaster farm. Jim left school in ninth grade to work for his father, but he wanted more contact with people than his farm work provided.

In nearby Paradise, Pennsylvania, Miriam "Mim" Hershey was also growing up on a Mennonite farm. She and her sister worked at a vegetable stand in Philadelphia on Saturdays. One of the products they sold was Utz Potato Chips.

Chips—and Mim—would soon become very important to Jim Herr. Looking to get into a business other than farming, in 1946 the twenty-one-year-old bought Verna's Potato Chips on Charlotte Street in Lancaster for $1,750. He renamed the operation Herr's Potato Chips. Jim packed the chips and sold them door-to-door. Mim, who was employed by a Lancaster attorney and who had met Jim a couple years previously, helped him out after her workday ended.

Things went well for the business and for the couple. They married in 1947, the same year that Herr's Potato Chips relocated to an empty tobacco barn on the Herr family farm. Two years later, the company needed more space, so Jim and Mim rented a 3,600-square-foot bakery in West Willow. The first of the Herrs' five children was also born in 1949. Around this time, Jim and Mim started teaching regularly at the Mount Vernon Mennonite Church in Oxford, about 25 miles from their home.

The family and the business were thriving, but on September 5, 1951, disaster struck. A fire completely destroyed the West Willow bakery. Fortunately, no one was inside, but the Herrs had to decide what to do next.

They chose to continue making potato chips and found a site in Nottingham, much closer to the church to which they had been commuting several times a week. They bought 37 acres for $18,000, built a 4,500-square-foot factory, and installed an automatic cooker. This site had another advantage: It was central to the markets of Philadelphia, West Chester, Wilmington, and Lancaster.

After surviving the potato shortage of 1952, Herr's Potato Chips got back on track. With the automatic cooker and a new heat exchanger, production increased to 130 pounds of chips per hour. Herr's chips were distributed to an increasingly wider geographic area and penetrated new markets like school cafeterias and the Woolworth chain. Jim Herr sold "allied products"—that is, other snacks—as part of his drive to be a full-service provider to his customers.

The next four and a half decades were years of expansion and innovation, punctuated occasionally with excitement such as the 1954 hurricane that tore off part of the roof and left Jim with broken ribs and a broken ankle. In 1963, the company officially incorporated as Herr's Potato Chips, Inc., and employees were offered a profit-sharing plan.

A milestone was reached in 1968, when annual sales exceeded $1 million for the first time. That year, Jim Herr was the president of the Eastern Regional Snack Food Association, and the following year, he was named Pennsylvania's Small Businessman of the Year by the U.S. Small Business Association.

There were several additions to the items Herr's manufactured: cheese curls in 1976, popcorn in 1978, corn and tortilla chips in 1983, and onion rings in 1984. The company name was changed in 1983 to Herr Foods, Inc., to reflect this diverse product line.

Through the years, Jim and Mim Herr maintained their strong faith and their commitment to family. Jim received permission to reprint a paraphrased version of the Book of Proverbs, which he has found especially helpful and meaningful. These little books, titled *Chips of Wisdom*, are available free of charge in the Herr's visitors center, but they are not forced upon anyone.

In 1981, all five of Jim and Mim's children were appointed to the company board of directors. Outsiders had warned against this, citing the possibility of family strife, but the Herrs have had no such problems. In 1989, Jim Herr turned the company presidency over to son J. M. Herr. Ten years later, Jim Herr's title was changed to founder and chairman, with J. M. being named chief executive officer and president.

Because of his experience in growing a small business into a large, successful operation, Jim was invited to join a presidential trade delegation on a trip to Japan, Singapore, Australia, and Korea in 1991. The following year, in Washington, he shared his insights with then-president Boris Yeltsin of Russia.

Herr Foods, Inc., quietly "does the right thing" in many ways, including recycling potato starch into paper, using wastewater from the plant to irrigate a nearby farm, buying back expired products and donating them to food banks, sharing its profits with employees, and adhering to a no-layoff policy. It's refreshing to find a large company that is also a good corporate citizen; this aspect of the company should give great satisfaction to the Herr family.

The Tour

So many people requested tours of the Herr's plant that the company built a 15,000-square-foot visitors center in 1989. Check in at the desk, and you'll be issued a ticket with the name of a Herr's product printed on it. While you wait for your tour to be called, you can have a snack in Chipper's Cafe (Chipper is the Herr's chipmunk mascot) or browse in the shop.

The tour begins with a ten-minute video shown in the 140-seat theater. It shares some company history and gives you a sneak peek of what you'll see in the factory.

Chipper the Chipmunk greets visitors in the gift shop.

Visiting Herr Foods

NOTTINGHAM, PA

Fax number: 610-932-4961

E-mail address:
Jennifer.Arrigo@herrs.com

Tour hours: Monday–Thursday,
9 A.M.–4 P.M.; Friday, 9 A.M.–noon
year-round. Closed weekends
and major holidays.

Admission: Free.

Reservations: Preferred. Call ahead
to avoid a wait. Groups must have
reservations.

Special considerations: No photography allowed. Specialized tours can be
given by prearrangement. Wheelchair
accessible, with elevator, ramps, and
low windows permitting views of the
factory operation. No age restrictions.
Strollers permitted.

Tour length and type: About 1 hour,
with a 10-minute introductory video
followed by a guided tour through galleries overlooking production areas.

Group size: Maximum of thirty per guide.
Individuals and families welcome.

On-site facilities: Gift and retail shop,
restrooms, picnic area, cafe.

Special events: Held throughout the
year; call for specifics. From Thanksgiving Day to New Year's Day, Herr's
has an outdoor Christmas light display
from dusk to dawn. Arrangements can
be made for birthday parties.

Nearby attractions: Contact the Chester
County Conference and Visitors
Bureau at 800-228-9933 or visit the
website www.brandywinevalley.com
for information about Southern
Chester County attractions, including
Brandywine Battlefield Park, the
Brandywine River Museum, Long-
wood Gardens, and Winterthur.

Directions: From the intersection of U.S.
1 and PA Route 272, take 272 south
very briefly. Turn right onto Herr Drive.
Follow signs; the route is well marked.

Your guide will then lead your group outside, past a pastoral mural of deer and a covered bridge. Herr's has thought of everything: If it's rain-ing, umbrellas are waiting at the door.

Into the pretzel room you go. Look through the glass, and you'll see dough mixed into 300-pound balls, then divided into more manageable 8-pound pieces. These go into an ex-truder that forces the dough through pretzel-shaped dies. Pretzels are baked in ovens heated to over 500 degrees. After baking, they dry in a kiln. The process is so highly automated that it takes only three people to run two pretzel rooms.

Then it's back outside for the trip to the gallery overlooking the corn room. The kernels are boiled for seven minutes, then soaked for eight hours. A pressure wash removes the hulls. The clean, soft corn is passed through a grinder that turns it into a thick paste. This is fed into a sheeter, a machine that cuts corn-chip shapes. Restaurant-style tortilla chips are baked, fried, and salted; regular tortilla chips skip the baking step. Some are tumbled in sea-soning, then go into a shaker that knocks off the excess.

The next two windows give views of the pretzel-packing area, where the pretzels are weighed, bagged, and boxed. You'll also see the corn-packing rooms, with form, fill, and seal machines. The former shapes film into bags. Weighed amounts of the product drop in, a puff of nitrogen removes oxygen, and the bag is sealed, date-stamped, and boxed.

Next, you'll visit the cheese curl and popcorn room. A video monitor supplements the guide's narrative.

And then it's time for everyone's favorite part of the tour: the potato chip production area. Ten truckloads of potatoes arrive every day and are washed, peeled, sliced, and rinsed. Next they're fried for three to five minutes in 350-degree vegetable oil. Cooked chips pass under a scanning machine that optically examines them for flaws. Air jets blow any chips with green or brown spots off the belt.

Your guide disappears behind a door, reemerging with a tray of warm chips fresh from the line. Everyone is happy to follow the company rule: You can't leave until the tray is empty.

Martin's Potato Chips

5847 Lincoln Highway West
Thomasville, PA 17364
717-792-3565 or 800-272-4477;
    ext. 3351 for tours
www.martinschips.com

When Harry Martin was a little boy, his parents had a stand at the farmer's market. In the next stall was the Utz family, selling homemade potato chips. Martin liked them so much that his mother fried her own for him at home. Hers were plenty tasty, too, and soon the Martins were also selling chips.

In 1941, Harry Martin and his wife, Fairy, outgrew the home kitchen, where they had continued making chips the same way Martin's mother had. The pair built a factory and expanded their distribution to include not only market stands, but also small grocery stores.

Thirty years later, Ken and Sandy Potter bought the business, retaining Martin family members as employees. The Potters' business plan was to expand outside the York area. By 1977, delivery routes covered York, Lancaster, Dauphin, and Adams Counties. As Martin's grew through the 1980s and 1990s, the company's success continued. Today, more than seventy routes operate from distribution facilities in Reading, Allentown, Philadelphia, and Williamsport, as well as Hagerstown, Maryland.

The company is primarily a regional one, but its management has consulted internationally. In 1985, Ken Potter helped open the first potato chip factory in China. He has also advised Australian snack company Arnott's Biscuits Ltd. and has offered similar help to a British firm.

Martin's remains a family operation. The Potters' three sons are active executives in the business: Ken Jr. is vice president of manufacturing, Kevin is vice president of sales, and David is a sales manager.

You might say that Martin's chips are presidential. They are proudly served aboard Air Force One.

The Tour
Martin's friendly tour lets you get right down on the factory floor to see the chip-making process. So put on that hair net and get ready for a fun and memorable experience.

Freshly peeled potatoes emerging from the peeler. Very large potatoes are cut in half by inspectors before travelling on to the slicer to be chipped.

Your guide will lead you outdoors, past a tank where 12,000 gallons of cooking oil is kept at 120 degrees so that it doesn't solidify. Listen for the sound of the pump moving the oil into the fryers.

Around the side of the building, trucks deliver 48,000-pound loads of potatoes, usually one or two shipments a day. To let the potatoes roll out smoothly, the entire truck is tilted gently up in the air. It's a spectacular sight to see a tractor-trailer at a 45-degree angle.

The spring harvest begins in March or April down south, with potatoes trucked up from Florida, then Georgia, then on up the East Coast. Upon arrival, each shipment undergoes a quality-control check before the spuds are unloaded: Chips are made from a random sample of potatoes to make sure the raw materials are up to Martin's standards.

Once the potatoes are approved, they're sent down a conveyor, where rubber rollers knock off the dirt. Your guide will lead you inside the building, where the hum of machinery tells you you're in a working factory. The potatoes are washed, then sent through a peeler. This handy machine is rough all around the inside, rubbing the peels off gently and efficiently. The parings aren't wasted; they're used for fertilizer. Every once in a while, conversation comes to a halt as another batch of potatoes thunders down the chute.

Next, the potatoes are inspected. Bad spots are cut off by hand, then the potatoes go through the slicing machine and into the fryer. For seven minutes, chips-to-be are immersed in hot oil. A worker with a rakelike tool beats them gently to keep the slices from sticking together. The next part of the process spins the potatoes around for a minute. A strategically placed mirror lets you see right into the spinner.

After a little jiggle down a conveyor belt, the chips are salted. Now it's time for a sample. They don't get any fresher than this. While you're munching, watch a single layer of fresh chips pass under an automatic picker. Anything with a dark spot is shot off the belt by a blast of air. A human also inspects the chips for any that are stuck together in clumps.

Buckets then hoist chips up to the packing area. Windows allow you to watch the packing process. Bags come flat on large rolls. A machine called a former creates the bags, and the product is dropped in. The jaw timing traps air in the bag to serve as a cushion to protect the chips during shipment. A machine stamps the price and date on each

While the sliced potatoes are frying, they are raked to keep them from sticking together.

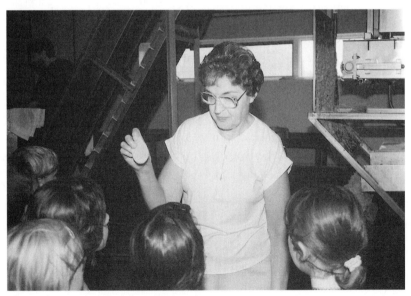

A tour guide has the complete attention of visitors. Many factory tour guides are experienced employees, who bring special knowledge and enthusiasm to the tour.

bag. Shelf life for a bag of chips is about eight weeks.

Up to six people work in the packing area, two at each of three packing machines. Boxes have to be assembled, packed, and closed. Sealed boxes are sent down a roller slide into the warehouse, where they're stacked on pallets.

Two things are striking at Martin's: how clean the operation is and how nice the people are. Staff members take the time to smile, say hi, and patiently wait for tour groups to get out of their way.

It's interesting to learn the ins and outs of delivery protocol. Route drivers returning with empty boxes break them down and place them on skids. Cartons can be used up to eight times before they're sent to the compactor for recycling. Drivers have their own pigeonholes, where they leave their orders. Warehouse personnel pull exactly what each driver needs. Each driver packs his or her own truck. That makes it easy to unload things in the right order along the route; it's similar to the efficiency you get when you bag your own groceries at the supermarket checkout.

If there's an empty trailer at the loading dock, you may be invited to go inside. You don't realize how big one of those things is until you've walked from one end to the other. Martin's operates more than seventy routes throughout central Penn-

Visiting Martin's
THOMASVILLE, PA

Fax number: 717-792-4906

Tour hours: Monday–Thursday, 8:30 A.M.–12:30 P.M. year-round.

Admission: Free.

Reservations: Groups must reserve at least a week in advance. Individuals and families should also reserve in advance. Walk-ins may be able to get a tour if a guide is available, but there are no guarantees.

Special considerations: Wheelchair accessible. No age restrictions. Strollers permitted. The tour goes through a working factory; wear closed-toed, nonskid shoes. Still and video cameras are permitted.

Tour length and type: 45 minutes to an hour. Guided tour of the factory floor.

Group size: Maximum of fifty per tour. Individuals and families welcome.

On-site facilities: Small factory store, restrooms.

Nearby attractions: Contact the York County Convention and Visitors Bureau at 888-858-YORK or visit the website www.yorkpa.org for information about attractions, including the Agricultural Museum of York County, Harley-Davidson Motorcycle Final Assembly Plant and Museum, the Historical Society Museum/York County Heritage Trust, and the York Barbell Museum and Weightlifting Hall of Fame. Wolfgang Candy Co. in York, Snyder's of Hanover, and Utz Quality Foods in Hanover also welcome visitors.

Directions: From the intersection of I-83 and U.S. Route 30 in York, take Route 30 West and go about 7 miles. Martin's Potato Chips is on the right, directly across the street from York Airport.

sylvania and northern Maryland, with distributors in Ohio and Virginia as well. Along with potato chips, Martin's makes popcorn at its 40,000-square-foot Thomasville facility; more than 1 million bags of snacks are produced each month. Martin's also distributes Wege Pretzels and a full line of locally made corn products.

Your tour ends at the retail counter, where you may purchase Martin's products. When you open your bag of Martin's potato chips back home, you'll know exactly how those chips were made.

Troyer Potato Products (Troyer Farms)

810 Route 97 South
Waterford, PA 16441
814-796-2611 or 800-458-0485
www.troyerfarms.com

If you wanted to make the freshest potato chips possible, you might do something like this: First you'd grow some of Pennsylvania's best chipping potatoes yourself. Then you'd build a potato chip processing plant right across the street from your fields. That's exactly what Troyer Farms has done. The result is an uncommonly fresh potato product that spells delight for consumers—and success for Troyer Farms.

It all started in the late 1930s, when farmer Dan Troyer left Nebraska in the wake of the Dust Bowl for northwestern Pennsylvania and began growing potatoes. Dan's farming expertise, combined with an ideal climate and soil type, led him to produce some of the most prized potatoes in the area.

Sons Clifford and Cletus Troyer, following in their father's footsteps, focused on growing top-quality chipping potatoes and selling them to manufacturers. In 1967, the brothers decided to make their own chips. They set up production lines and established three delivery routes.

That small operation has expanded steadily, thanks in large part to creative thinking by the Troyer family, which still owns and runs the business. For example, when the 1978 energy crisis halted production for weeks and threatened the company with a complete shutdown (as a "nonessential" food processor, Troyer Farms was not exempt from

An aerial view of Troyer Farms factory and the surrounding potato fields.
COURTESY OF TROYER POTATO PRODUCTS, INC.

rationing), the Troyers decided to drill their own natural gas wells rather than convert to prohibitively expensive fuel oil.

By 1983, the company had eighty-five routes. In 1984, Troyer acquired the Cleveland-based Dan Dee Pretzel and Potato Chip Company and consolidated Dan Dee's manufacturing into the Waterford plant. This expansion enabled the company to penetrate the Ohio market rapidly.

Troyer is unique in that it is the only Pennsylvania chip maker that grows its own spuds. With more than 2,000 acres of farmland, 900 of which is for potatoes, Troyer Farms supplies its 325,000-square-foot Waterford plant from mid-July through November. The 20 million pounds of homegrown potatoes are just over half of the company's annual consumption. By controlling potato variety, fertilizing, harvest, and handling, the company manages some of the variables that affect potato quality.

Low-Fat Chips

Chip manufacturers have been wrestling with the problem of how to get the fat out of potato chips without destroying their texture and taste. Some have opted to use a fat substitute, Olestra, but Troyer Potato Products has taken a different approach. The company has entered into a joint venture agreement with Supernatural Foods of Baton Rouge, Louisiana, which developed a patented process to extract fat from salted snacks after they have been fried in vegetable oil the usual way.

When a 400-pound batch of chips destined for low-fatdom comes out of the fryer, it is placed into a vessel filled with a food-grade solvent. The length of time the chips stay in the vessel determines whether the chips will be reduced-fat or fat-free. A twenty-minute bath is enough for low-fat chips; it takes a bit longer to make them fat-free. The reduced-fat chips have just 2 grams of fat and 80 calories per nineteen-chip serving, compared with 12 grams of fat and 150 calories in the regular chips.

Once the fat is reduced to the desired level, the solution of solvent and oil goes to a separating vessel, where the solvent vaporizes. Defatted chips are removed from the vessel, loaded onto a conveyor belt, and transported to a packaging machine.

Darrel Troyer expects the new low-fat product to make up about 5 to 10 percent of the market. So far, the response has been positive. Troyer Potato Products also plans to add new flavors of low-fat chips soon and is researching the possibility of defatting other snack products.

For optimum freshness, Troyer minimizes the time between digging and processing. It's not unusual for a potato that was dug in early morning to be turned into chips and bagged by lunchtime.

Potatoes can't be grown year-round in Erie County, however. After the local harvest is finished, the Troyers store the rest of their crop in million-pound bins under strictly controlled environmental conditions. Starting in April, newly harvested potatoes from Florida arrive, followed by fresh spuds from other states, moving north up the East Coast. By early or mid-July, harvesting begins again on Troyer Farms.

Inside the factory, a highly automated process indicates the firm's willingness to invest in state-of-the-art processing and packaging equipment. Troyer Farms spent more than $7 million in a three-year period to increase production and efficiency. From motorized conveyors to automatic case packers to robotic palletizers to high-speed form-fill-seal machines capable of handling up to 120 bags a minute, this investment in automation has been a key part of the company's growth and prosperity. The forward-thinking Troyer Farms team is also considering other ways to distribute its products, including private label and food service opportunities.

The list of management personnel shows how important family is at Troyer Farms. Clifford Troyer is president, as he has been since the company's inception; Darrel Troyer is vice president of sales and marketing; Mark Troyer is vice president of transportation and farming; Craig Troyer serves as vice president and regional sales manager; Steve Troyer handles the controller's job. Many other family members work in the organization. (Cletus sold his part to his brother and is no longer a partner.)

Today, Troyer Farms is thriving, with over 200 company routes and 45 owner-operator routes. Its two plants, this one in Waterford and another in Canonsburg, combine to produce and distribute potato chips, popcorn, tortilla chips, pretzels, and extruded snacks such as cheese twists and corn puffs. Dan Troyer would no doubt be proud that his move to Pennsylvania

A cascade of cooked chips is dispensed into chutes to be weighed and dropped into bags.
COURTESY OF TROYER POTATO PRODUCTS, INC.

Visiting Troyer's
WATERFORD, PA

Fax number: 814-796-6757

E-mail address: info@troyerfarms.com

Tour hours: Monday–Thursday, 8:30, 9:30, and 10:30 A.M., and 1, 2, and 3 P.M., May through October. Tours also can be arranged by appointment.

Admission: Free.

Reservations: Required. Contact tour director at 814-796-2611 or 800-458-0485, ext. 131.

Special considerations: Not wheelchair accessible. No age restrictions. Strollers permitted, but they must be carried up a flight of steps. Still cameras permitted, although it's difficult to take photographs through the wire-reinforced gallery windows. No video cameras allowed.

Tour length and type: 45 minutes to an hour. Twelve-minute video presentation and live introduction by tour guide, then guided tour through gallery overlooking processing areas.

Group size: Maximum of sixty people. Individuals and families welcome.

On-site facilities: Small retail kiosk, restrooms.

Nearby attractions: Contact the Erie Area Convention and Visitors Bureau at 800-542-ERIE or visit the website www.eriepa.com for information about Erie attractions, including the Erie Art Museum, Erie Historical Museum, Erie Maritime Museum and U.S. Brig *Niagara*, Presque Isle State Park, Waldameer Park and Water World, and wineries. Pulakos 926 Chocolates on Parade Street also welcomes visitors.

Directions: From I-90, take Exit 6 for Peach Street/U.S. Route 19 South. Continue on 19 South for approximately 10 miles to Waterford. Go through Waterford, then take PA Route 97 South. Troyer Farms is on the right in about 1.5 miles.

has had such a profitable and enduring legacy.

The Tour

Your tour begins even before you reach the factory, with views of Troyer's verdant potato fields near the plant. In the parking lot, the smell of frying potatoes wafts through the air. Guests who happen to arrive at unloading time are treated to the awesome sight of a tractor-trailer tilted at an almost 45-degree angle on a huge lift as it dispenses some of the 500,000 pounds of potatoes that Troyer Farms uses each day.

Inside, a tour guide escorts you up a flight of stairs from a small lobby to a sixty-seat theater for a twelve-minute video presentation. The film, starring the perky "Miss Keri Crinkle" on a tractor in the Troyer potato patch, relates the history of the three-generation family business. When the tape concludes, the guide displays a cornucopia of packaged Troyer products, acquainting visitors with the company's complete line of snacks.

The guide shares some impressive numbers: Troyer Farms makes 5,000 pounds of potato chips per hour, which translates to 250,000 bags per day, in a fryer that holds 2,500 gallons of oil. Each hour, the factory also produces 1,500 pounds of tortilla chips, 1,800 pounds of extruded products (corn puffs or cheese puffs), and 1,000 pounds of popcorn. The guide also explains the potato chip production process, from the time the potatoes reach the factory to the time the chips finish cooking.

Next, it's off to the gallery windows overlooking the production floor. A fascinating process it is. Once the potatoes are unloaded, they're tumbled in a machine with abrasive material on the inside to peel them in a flash. They're washed, then conveyed to an inspector, who manually cuts off any bad spots. A slicing machine then cuts each spud into about twenty slices. The slices are rinsed to remove excess starch, then they are slipped into the fryer, which moves them from one end to the other as they cook for two and a half minutes. The cooked chips pass under a salter, then through a machine that optically inspects them for dark spots. Rejects are blown off the conveyor belt by automatic air jets. Dark chips aren't discarded; they make satisfactory animal feed.

The packaging process is equally interesting. Chips are fed into scales, then dropped into newly formed bags. After the bags are closed, they undergo a pressure and seal check. If a bag fails, the chips are sent back to be rebagged; the defective packaging is discarded. Satisfactory bags continue to the case packer, where they are collated, counted, and boxed.

Depending on what else is being produced that day, you may also see big blobs of masa, or corn flour, being formed into tortilla chips; extruded snacks puffing up to their finished size; and snacks passing through flavor drums to get an even coating of spices.

The tour concludes with a stop at a small stand where Troyer products are for sale at discount prices. Snack-size bags of chips or other treats are given to each guest, and the guide often serves a tray of snacks, too. After tasting the fresh chips, visitors agree with the Troyer Farms motto: "Simply better."

Utz Quality Foods

900 High Street
Hanover, PA 17331
717-637-6644 or 800-367-7629
www.utzsnacks.com

Bill Utz was a shoe factory worker with entrepreneurial dreams back in 1921, when he heard that a man in York had potato chip–making equipment to sell. Bill talked things over with his wife, Salie, who agreed to help with the new venture. They scraped together $300 and bought the equipment.

Their friends told them they were crazy.

Their friends were wrong.

Salie set up the hand-operated equipment in the kitchen of the couple's home on McAllister Street in Hanover and used her Pennsylvania Dutch cooking skills and work ethic to produce 50 pounds of chips per hour. Bill was in charge of deliveries. His territory included independent stores and farmers markets in and around the Hanover area. They also sold the chips at local fairs, which most towns had in those days.

Bill had been right about the market possibilities. Demand increased such that Salie and Bill built a separate factory building behind their house. The addition of an automatic chip cooker in 1936 boosted their production up to 300 pounds per hour. Son-in-law F. X. "Xav" Rice came on board to manage business operations.

Things continued to go well. In 1949, a 68,000-square-foot plant was built on a 10-acre site on Carlisle Street in Hanover. Before the founders died—Salie in 1965 and Bill three years later—six additions expanded the plant to 265,000 square feet. Xav Rice became the president of the company. He continued the strong family leadership that was the company's backbone since its inception.

Major growth continued. In 1971, the company purchased and renovated a plant on Broadway in Hanover, adding pretzels to the product mix. Popcorn production was begun at that plant a few years later.

*William and Salie Utz, the founders of Hanover Home Brand
Potato Chips, later known as Utz Quality Foods, Inc.* COURTESY
OF UTZ QUALITY FOODS, INC., AND GRAPHICS PLUS

Utz expanded from its base as the top chip in Baltimore and south-central Pennsylvania into the rest of Maryland and Washington, D.C. With the opening of a 50,000-square-foot plant on High Street in 1976, production capacity reached 7,000 pounds of chips per hour. The market area continued to expand, encompassing Delaware, Virginia, and West Virginia by the late 1970s.

Xav Rice retired in 1978, and his son Mike took over. The third generation of family management innovated as aggressively as previous generations had. Utz installed in-truck computers for inventory management, invoice preparation, and account transaction processing. The company greatly expanded its distribution through twenty-one distribution centers designed solely for Utz. Its full line of snack products is now sold as far north as Massachusetts and as far south as North Carolina. Pretzels are distributed nationwide through mass merchandisers such as Sam's Club, Price Costco, and B. J.'s. Through mail order, Utz products are sent all over the United States, as well as overseas.

The High Street plant has grown as well and now covers more than 800,000 square feet. More than 14,000 pounds of potato chips are produced every hour, along with corn chips and tortilla chips.

See what can happen when you follow your dream?

The Tour

Utz Quality Foods' High Street facility invites visitors to learn about the company's history and to watch the production process in action. As you enter, you'll see company memorabilia, including old posters, tins, product packages, trade magazine articles, even Grandpa Bill Utz's glasses case.

Turn the corner, and you'll find yourself in an elevated, glass-fronted viewing area overlooking the factory floor. Your observations are supplemented by an audio program and video monitors. Some of these stations are fairly close together, so it's best to hang back and allow the people in front of you to move ahead slightly. That lessens the possibility that you'll hear the audio from two different stations at once. Youngsters can get a better view by standing on the ramps. When you're ready, press the button on the wall. Some twinkly music will alert you that the narrative is about to begin.

As you progress through the tour, you'll learn that Utz's basic potato chips are made from just three ingredients: potatoes, oil, and salt. Most of the chips are fried in cottonseed oil, but the Grandma Utz brand is kettle-cooked in refined lard, and Kettle Classics are hand-cooked in peanut oil. It takes just a half hour to turn a raw potato into finished chips.

Chipping potatoes, either freshly dug or from the up to 40 million pounds stored in Utz's temperature- and humidity-controlled cellars, are sorted by size, washed, and peeled. Then they're sliced to a precise .055

Visiting Utz Quality Foods
HANOVER, PA

Fax number: 717-637-3756

E-mail: pberwager@utzsnacks.com

Tour hours: Observation gallery open Monday–Thursday, 7:30 A.M.–4:30 P.M. Factory outlet store open Monday–Saturday, 8:00 A.M.–7 P.M.; Sunday, 11 A.M.–6 P.M. Both open year round.

Admission: Free.

Reservations: Required for groups of ten or more.

Special considerations: Guided wheelchair tours. No age restrictions. Strollers permitted. No photography permitted. Retail store about a quarter mile away.

Tour length and type: About 45 minutes. Self-guided for individuals and families; guided for groups of ten or more. A short film is shown before you enter the observation gallery.

Group size: No maximum number of people per tour. Individuals and families welcome.

On-site facilities: Restrooms.

Nearby attractions: Contact the York County Convention and Visitors Bureau at 888-858-YORK or visit the website www.yorkpa.org for information about attractions, including the Agricultural Museum of York County, Harley-Davidson Motorcycle Final Assembly Plant and Museum, the Historical Society Museum/York County Heritage Trust, and the York Barbell Museum and Weightlifting Hall of Fame. Snyder's of Hanover, Wolfgang Candy Co. in York, and Martin's Potato Chips in Thomasville also welcome visitors.

Directions: From the Square in Hanover, turn onto PA Route 94 North (Carlisle Street). At the traffic light at Clearview Road, you'll see an Utz plant on your right. For the factory outlet store, turn right; the store's on the right. For the factory tour, turn left onto Clearview Road. At the next stop sign, turn left again onto High Street, then make an immediate right. The building and parking lot are on your right.

Outlet store:
861 Carlisle Street
Hanover, Pennsylvania 17331
800-367-7629

inches thick. Spud slices are tumbled through fresh water to remove starch. This makes the finished chips lighter in color and texture.

Frying comes next. The chips go into 340-degree cooking oil for about two and a half minutes while rotating paddle wheels keep them from clumping together. Out comes the moisture, in stay the nutrients. Utz's five stainless steel frying lines produce thirteen thousand finished chips per hour. Cooked chips are inspected, and any that have dark spots—caused by a concentration of reducing sugars in the potato—are removed. The survivors are lightly salted.

As the chips move up a conveyor belt, they cool to room temperature. Watch them jiggle along, propelled by rapid vibration. About 30

The visitor's view: the bagging and packing stage. COURTESY OF UTZ QUALITY
FOODS, INC., AND GRAPHICS PLUS

percent of the chips will be seasoned in tumblers that apply spices
evenly on the chip surface.

Move along and you'll see more than thirty form, fill, and seal machines. These are really fun to watch. Utz bags chips in packages ranging
from half an ounce to 4 pounds. Chips fill each hopper until the weight
is correct, then the bottom of the scale section opens right over an open
bag. In go the chips. A blast of nitrogen flushes oxygen out of the bag,
which helps keep the chips fresh. Bags are sealed, boxed, and placed on
plastic pallets.

At the next station, you'll get some information about the warehouse, which provides short-term storage for over 150 products and package styles. Maximum purity and freshness is the goal. To that end, Utz employs a first-in, first-out product rotation, has air-conditioned its warehouse space, and runs its forklift trucks on battery power, not propane. An in-floor tow-line conveyor system moves the product with minimal human intervention.

Utz is justifiably proud of its tightly run distribution system. No Utz product goes through a broker warehouse. By directly controlling the entire distribution chain, the company is able to deliver chips efficiently. Ninety percent of Utz chips are consumed within a week of their manufacture. On your way out after the tour, pick up a free sample so that you can taste the freshness yourself.

PRETZELS

What do you think the Pilgrims snacked on during their 1620 journey on the Mayflower? It wasn't cranberry sauce. It was probably pretzels, and they've been popular in the New World ever since.

Pennsylvania has been a perennial hub of pretzel activity. From Anderson to Wege and everything in between, the state boasts a plethora of pretzel manufacturers, several of which offer tours. This stems in large part from the love that the original Pennsylvania Dutch—or German—settlers had for pretzels. Children wore them on strings around their necks on New Year's Day for good luck.

It was a Pennsylvania Dutchman, Julius Sturgis, who opened the first commercial pretzel bakery in America. You can visit the birthplace of the nation's pretzel industry in Lititz, Lancaster County, where the Sturgis Pretzel House is a historic site as well as an active pretzel bakery.

Soft pretzels are ubiquitous in nearby Philadelphia. From pushcarts and roadside stands to athletic events and festivals, the generously salted, figure-eight-shaped treats are sold everywhere. Ask for extra napkins, because you have to eat them slathered with mustard.

Philadelphians' love for pretzels doesn't stop with the soft variety. Nationally, the average annual consumption of hard pretzels is about $1^1/_2$ to 2 pounds per person; Philadelphians eat twelve times that amount.

Anyone who has been to a shopping mall in the last decade likely has seen an Auntie Anne's pretzel stand. Anne Beiler opened her first Auntie Anne's Hand-Rolled Soft Pretzels stand in a farmers' market in Downingtown, Chester County, in 1988. Today there are more than six hundred Auntie Anne's locations around the world. Dough is still made fresh in each store using a proprietary recipe, then rolled by hand and baked.

In many Auntie Anne's franchises, you can see pretzel making done the old-fashioned way. For a closer, hands-on experience, visit Sturgis

Opposite: Pretzels made the old-fashioned way at Sturgis Pretzel House.

Pretzel House and Intercourse Pretzel Factory. The latter is also the home of a unique stuffed pretzel. You can watch pretzel making with modern machinery at Anderson Bakery Company and Snyder's of Hanover.

No matter which factory you visit, you're sure to enjoy the free sample you're offered after your tour. Welcome to Pretzelvania!

Anderson Bakery Company (Anderson Pretzels)

2060 Old Philadelphia Pike
Lancaster, PA 17602-3497
717-299-2321
www.andersonpretzel.com

The history of Anderson Bakery Company mirrors American industrial progress over the past century or so. Like the rest of the country's manufacturing practices, production methods at Anderson changed during that period from manual to mechanized, with corresponding increases in yield. The factory tour at Anderson offers a chance for you to see some photographic documentation of the company's evolution and to enjoy impressive views of snack making the twenty-first-century way.

The bakery was started in 1888 by a Mr. Eichler—nobody seems to remember his first name—at 336 North Charlotte Street in Lancaster. Eichler took on Bill Anderson as a partner sometime before World War I. Eichler later left the business, and Anderson's son Herbert became a partner. In the 1920s, Herbert named the company the H. K. Anderson Bakery.

Back in those days, pretzels were twisted by hand. A wooden peel—a large, flat, wooden spatula with a long handle, like you might see in a pizza parlor—was used to put uncooked pretzels into the brick oven and to remove them when they were done. Eight employees working all day could make about 500 pounds of pretzels.

A big improvement was the installation of the company's first rotary oven in 1949. It included a device that pulled finished pretzels out of the oven, leaving the baker free to feed raw pretzels in. By 1953, an automatic cooking system made even that unnecessary. Hand twisting ended in 1955, when the company installed six twisting machines. This equipment allowed the company to produce a competitively priced product and to expand its business.

When the Charlotte Street location could no longer keep up with demand, the bakery moved to 245 Ranck Avenue in Lancaster. This plant housed Anderson's first straight tunnel oven.

In 1971, the bakery moved to its current location. The tunnel oven from Ranck Avenue was moved, and a second one was added. One line was equipped with twisting machines, while the second made pretzels by extrusion. As the business grew, more ovens were installed. Currently, Anderson has seven oven lines at this location. The headquarters building is approximately 140,000 square feet; about 260 people work here.

In 1986, Anderson purchased a second plant in nearby New Holland. That facility started with one oven. Now, the 24,000-square-foot plant has three ovens and thirty employees.

Anderson now runs three daily shifts, and its ten ovens can crank out more than 100,000 pounds in one eight-hour shift. That's a two hundred-fold increase from production levels in 1946.

Pretzels at Anderson come in many shapes: traditional, thick Bavarian Dutch style, thin, miniature, party shapes, sticks, rods, gems, and logs. There are a variety of flavors, too, including plain, honey mustard, peanut butter filled, and baldies, which are unsalted.

The pretzels go into bags, boxes, cartons, and tins in amounts up to 18 pounds. The company packs pretzels under two of its own labels, Anderson and National, and also under hundreds of private labels. These pretzels,

Cooked pretzels are weighed and bagged.

A Twisted History

I'll bet you can't trace your family tree as far back as the pretzel can. The crunchy treat that we take for granted today has a long and illustrious history. It was in the year 610 A.D., at a monastery in Southern France or Northern Italy, that a creative monk first formed strips of bread dough into the shape of a child's arms folded in prayer. The three holes represented the Christian Trinity. The warm, doughy tidbit was given to children who had memorized their Bible verses and prayers. It was called *pretiola*, Latin for "little reward." The *pretiola* journeyed beyond the French and Italian wine regions, crossed the Alps, spread through Austria, and moved into Germany, where it became known as the bretzel or pretzel.

The spiritual significance of pretzels continued and expanded. In 1440, a page in the prayer book used by Catharine of Cleves depicted St. Bartholomew surrounded by pretzels. Pretzels were thought to foster spiritual wholeness.

Mid-fourteenth-century Germans ate pretzels and hard-boiled eggs for dinner on Good Friday. The pretzel symbolized everlasting life; two eggs, nestled in the pretzel's round holes, represented rebirth.

Pretzels were even included in marriage ceremonies. The expression "tying the knot" may have originated in Switzerland in the early 1600s, when royal couples used a pretzel as a nuptial knot. After that, it was common for couples to wish on a pretzel at their weddings. The bride would pull on one side, the groom on the other, wishbone-style; the one ending up with the larger piece would get his or her wish.

all of the same high quality as the products that bear the Anderson name, are packaged for grocery stores, drugstores, mass merchandisers, diet centers, and warehouse clubs.

The Tour

As you enter the Anderson building, pick up an information sheet before heading to the second floor to start your tour. You'll probably find the views so interesting that you won't want to read the pamphlet then

Like many wonderful inventions, the hard pretzel was first made by accident. One young baker fell asleep as his pretzels baked. He woke up and realized that the fire had died down. Suspecting that his pretzels hadn't been baked enough, he stoked the fire and let them cook twice as long as usual.

What the baker found when he removed the pretzels from the oven was not the soft, doughy kind he was used to, but something that had been toasted to a crisp, crunchy brown. The "overbaked" product was sampled, and it soon caught on. An added advantage of the hard pretzel was its low moisture content. Unlike soft pretzels, which lasted only a day or two, hard pretzels could be stored for months.

As the years passed, not much changed in the pretzel production department. Then, in the twentieth century, modern machinery revolutionized the way pretzels were made. Hand twisting gave way to automatic twisting machines, then extruders, which force the dough through a pretzel-shaped die and cut it off when it's the right size.

Extrusion is a very efficient process, producing between 1,000 and 1,200 pounds of pretzels per hour compared with the 600 pounds or so a mechanical twisting machine can make. Still, some manufacturers, like Utz Quality Foods, make at least some of their products on mechanical twisters, because this process puts less stress and pressure on the dough.

There's nothing like watching pretzels being twisted by hand, though, and nothing like trying it yourself. You can still do both at Sturgis Pretzel House and at Intercourse Pretzel Factory. When you're done, you'll have earned your own *pretiola*, a little reward for your efforts.

and there, but you can glance at it for some quick facts while you're on-site and read the rest later at your leisure.

The first exhibits are photographs of the old days. Black-and-white pictures of employees hand-packing boxes, filling trays, and twisting pretzels give the feel of what things used to be like. More recent photos show Anderson's headquarters and its New Holland plant, a letter from then-governor Robert P. Casey on the occasion of Anderson's centennial anniversary, and packaged products.

Visiting Anderson Bakery Company

LANCASTER, PA

Fax number: 717-393-3511

E-mail address: Through website, www.andersonpretzel.com

Tour hours: Monday–Friday, 8:30 A.M.–4 P.M. year-round. No tours on holidays. Retail store open Monday–Friday 8:30 A.M.–5 P.M. year-round; Saturday 8:30 A.M.–3 P.M. April–December; holidays 8:30 A.M.–5 P.M., except Thanksgiving, Christmas, and New Year's. Hours subject to change.

Admission: Free.

Reservations: Helpful.

Special considerations: Wheelchair accessible, with an elevator to the second-floor gallery. No age restrictions. Strollers permitted. Still and video cameras permitted. Glass windows make flash photography difficult; if you can get enough light and keep your camera steady, you can get good pictures without a flash.

Tour length and type: 15 to 20 minutes. Self-guided.

Group size: No maximum number of people. Individuals and families welcome.

On-site facilities: Factory store, restrooms.

Nearby atractions: Contact the Pennsylvania Dutch Convention and Visitors Bureau at 800-PA-DUTCH or visit the website www.padutchcountry.com for information about Lancaster-area attractions, including Dutch Wonderland family amusement park, Ephrata Cloister, factory outlets, James Buchanan's Wheatland, Landis Valley Museum, National Watch and Clock Museum, Railroad Museum of Pennsylvania, Strasburg Railroad Company, wineries, and more. The Intercourse Canning Company and the Intercourse Pretzel Factory, in Intercourse, also welcome visitors, as do several sites in Lititz: the Cake And Kandy Emporium, Sturgis Pretzel House, and Wilbur Chocolate Candy Americana Museum & Store.

Directions: From the intersection of U.S. Route 30 and PA Route 340, take Route 340 East. Anderson Pretzels is on the right in about a quarter mile.

You can feel the vibrations from the factory below. Large windows afford great views of the pretzel-making process from start to finish. Crossbeams in the hallway are labeled with information about what you're looking at; these correspond to the headings on your printed sheet.

First you see the basic ingredients of Anderson pretzels—wheat flour, water, corn syrup, malt, vegetable shortening, yeast, and salt—being mixed into dough. These ingredients come through pipes from their bulk storage tanks. You'll get a peek at one of the company's four large mixers. Batches of dough are mixed in weights varying from 300 to 850 pounds, depending upon the item being mixed and the equipment used. Mixed dough is transported either automatically by conveyors or on a dough cart to the production line.

Next, you get to see how extruded products are made. Either the dough gets dumped into a hopper automatically or a worker with a long, sharp knife hacks hunks of it from a container, then tosses it into the receiving end of the machine. The dough is pushed through openings in a metal die. After the right amount is forced through, sharp blades cut it off, and the resulting piece falls into place on a conveyor.

Pretzels then go onto the proof belt, which takes them into the oven room. During their journey, the yeast in the pretzels raises, or proofs, the dough. Proofed pretzels get dipped in a hot soda solution, which gives them their brown color. Still wet from the cooker, the pretzels are salted, then cooked in ovens set at 400 to 550 degrees F. Anderson's ovens range from 120 feet long to 200, thought to be the longest pretzel oven in the United States.

After baking, pretzels drop into the drying kilns, where their moisture level is reduced. Then they are taken to the form, fill, and seal machines. Pretzels are dispensed into scales. When the right weight is measured, that amount is dropped into a waiting bag underneath. Bags are sealed, packed in cartons, and placed on pallets that will transport them to the shipping area. Up to twelve trailers can be loaded at once. These take Anderson pretzels all over North America. You don't have to travel far to get your own pretzel; head down to the retail store to try a fresh sample.

Intercourse Pretzel Factory

3614 Old Philadelphia Pike
Intercourse, PA 17534
717-768-3432

It's nice to know that in a world of megaconglomerates and mass production, there's still a niche for a small manufacturing concern. One such "little guy" is Intercourse Pretzel Factory, where the pretzels are hand-twisted, the taste is traditional, and the focus is on quality, not quantity.

You'd never suspect that there was a factory in the middle of the Cross Keys Village Center, a small shopping area that includes gift shops, specialty food stores, and furniture stores. From the outside, Intercourse Pretzel Factory looks like any other store. Even when you go inside, the retail space doesn't give a clue about the manufacturing that takes place on the premises.

In the front, a variety of items with a local heritage are for sale. Pretzels are prevalent, of course, both the hard variety—in plain, herb, cheese, or brown butter flavors—and the soft version. Visitors are welcome to enjoy their treats at the tables.

One goody that's worth trying is a unique food product invented at Intercourse Pretzel Factory: the stuffed pretzel. Soft pretzel dough is rolled out and filled with local meats, cheeses, jams, and relishes. There are eighteen varieties, including the Pennsylvania Dutch Reuben with smoked sweet bologna instead of corned beef, sausage and pepper relish "pretzelwich," Philadelphia cheesesteak, and pepperoni pizza.

Intercourse Pretzel Factory also sells chocolate-covered pretzels coated in rich, premium-quality Wilbur chocolate, each with more than half its weight in chocolate. The molasses caramel crunch sold here is nirvana for fans of buttery "brown" food. It contains sweet, brown caramel tossed with dark roasted peanuts from Ephrata, molasses from Honeybrook, fresh popped corn, and pretzels made on site.

The store also sells jams, bulk herbs and spices, antiques, candy and fudge, ice cream, coffee, and hand-squeezed lemonade.

The Tour

Check in at the counter, and you'll be invited to take a tour behind the scenes. When you enter the manufacturing area, you'll smell something delightfully yeasty and moist. Inhale deeply as you take your place at the long purple counter that overlooks the manufacturing floor. Watch the workers in action while the guide explains the pretzel-making process. They nonchalantly roll the dough, grab the ends, lift it up and flip it around, then drop the resulting pretzel shape onto a baking sheet at precisely the right moment.

Looks easy, right? Now it's your turn. Everyone gets a piece of pretzel dough to practice on. Shaping the pretzel isn't especially hard, but that flick of the wrists is a bit tricky. The efforts of the novice pretzel makers on

Visiting Intercourse Pretzel Factory

INTERCOURSE, PA

Mailing address: P.O. Box 377, Intercourse, PA 17534.

Fax number: 717-768-0240

Tour hours: Tuesday–Saturday, 9 A.M.–3 P.M. Easter–Columbus Day; also open the same hours Monday in July and August. The rest of the year, open Saturdays, 9 A.M.–3 P.M., and during the week by chance. Retail store open February 15–December 31, Monday–Saturday, 9 A.M.–5 P.M.

Admission: Free.

Reservations: Required for groups of fifteen or more.

Special considerations: Wheelchair accessible. No age restrictions. Strollers permitted. Absolutely no photos may be taken of the staff. Visitors may photograph each other twisting pretzels. Pretzel making is weather dependent. When it's hot and humid, the dough picks up too much moisture. Call ahead to see if pretzels are in production.

Tour length and type: 15 minutes. Guide discusses pretzels, pretzel making, and the factory. You can watch pretzels being hand-twisted in the area below. Everyone gets a chance to twist a pretzel.

Group size: Maximum of fifty people. Individuals and families welcome.

On-site facilities: Retail store with antiques, bulk spices, pretzels, sandwiches; small seating area, restrooms.

Nearby attractions: Contact the Pennsylvania Dutch Convention and Visitors Bureau at 800-PA-DUTCH or visit the website www.padutchcountry.com for information about Lancaster-area attractions, including Dutch Wonderland family amusement park, Ephrata Cloister, factory outlets, James Buchanan's Wheatland, Landis Valley Museum, National Watch and Clock Museum, Railroad Museum of Pennsylvania, Strasburg Railroad Company, wineries, candle making, and more. Intercourse Canning Company is just across Newport Road. Anderson Bakery Company (Anderson Pretzels) in Lancaster also welcomes visitors, as do several sites in Lititz: the Cake And Kandy Emporium, Sturgis Pretzel House, and Wilbur Chocolate Candy Americana Museum & Store.

Directions: Located at the intersection of PA Route 340 and PA Route 772 East in the village of Intercourse in Cross Keys Village Center. The building is in a small shopping center and does not look like a factory.

either side of me ended up in a misshapen heap as often as mine did. Fortunately, dough is forgiving, so you get to try again. Roll your dough nice and long, position your hands close to the counter surface when you lift and twist, and keep a smile on your face. Before you know it, you'll be the proud recipient of a sticker that brands you an Official Pretzel Twister.

The guide explains that as a small bakery, Intercourse Pretzel Factory produces about 100 pounds of pretzels each day; that's less than two thousand pretzels. The dough is the same for soft and for hard pretzels.

Once the unsalted dough is mixed, shaped pretzels are bathed in a solution of sodium hydroxide and water. This gives them a rich, brown color and adds a flavor contrast to the inside taste. After a ten-second dip in the 180-degree liquid, the pretzels are baked for nine to twelve minutes. At this point, they're soft pretzels. Because of their moisture content, soft pretzels last only a day. For that reason, they're not shipped, but can only be purchased at the Intercourse store.

To make hard pretzels, the soft pretzels are baked again, in an oven set on low heat for an hour and fifteen minutes. These hard pretzels are bagged and labeled, and will stay fresh for up to eight months.

Snyder's of Hanover

1250 York Street
Hanover, PA 17331
717-632-4477 or 800-233-7125
www.snydersofhanover.com

Snyder's of Hanover has always set high goals and has achieved them. From its simple beginnings selling homemade edibles to its global presence today, the company has been a stellar performer in the snack food arena. The company mission statement reads, in part, "To ensure customer satisfaction by assuring we produce and pack the best quality bag possible through efficiencies, teamwork and communication as we strive to become the #1 snack food company in the world." After touring the Snyder's of Hanover plant and learning a little about the company's history, you get the feeling that there's a good chance Snyder's will fulfill that ambition.

Snyder's Bakery was begun in 1924 by William V. Snyder and his wife, Helen, who made and sold angel food cakes and egg noodles. It made perfect sense for them to produce two such seemingly diverse items: With characteristic Pennsylvania Dutch thrift, the Snyders used egg whites in their cakes and the yolks in their noodles.

In the 1930s, sons William V. Jr. and Edward joined the family business. They added potato chips to the expanding product line, and the company thrived in the 1940s. An automated chip line was built at the original Granger Street factory in Hanover. In 1946, Snyder's Bakery was incorporated. By 1948, the Hanover location had been doubled in size, to 10,000 square feet; the Snyders opened a second plant in Berlin, Pennsylvania, near a good supply of potatoes and the growing Pittsburgh market.

William V. Snyder died in 1949. Subsequently, the Berlin plant was sold to his sister Edith Sterner and her husband, Barb, who operated it until 1973.

Meanwhile, the Hanover plant was operated under a trust for William's son until 1961. It was then sold to Hanover Foods Corporation, owned by the Warehimes, who had been in the pretzel-making business since 1909, when Harry V. Warehime started the Hanover Pretzel Company with a single recipe, Hanover Olde Tyme Pretzels. Hanover Foods Corporation changed the name of the company from Snyder's Bakery to Hanover Guest Quality Food Corporation, stopped making egg noodles, and continued marketing other products under the Snyder's label. In 1962, the company also bought the distribution company belonging to Edward Snyder Jr. and his son, Edward III, which consisted of five routes. This was the beginning of the company's distribution system.

In 1963, Hanover Foods Corporation company purchased the Bechtel Pretzel Company and began producing the product that would soon become the company's top seller, using the delicious pretzel recipe that had been in the family since 1909. The Snyder's Sourdough Hard Pretzel is perennially the runaway winner in the domestic hard pretzel market.

Snyder's of Hanover has a factory store that you can visit after you take the tour.

Chip and pretzel manufacturing became increasingly automated, and the company broadened its distribution territory to include central Pennsylvania, Baltimore, and Washington, D.C. By 1969, products from Hanover were penetrating the Pittsburgh market. This caused a conflict with the Snyder company based in Berlin, because that company was also selling snack foods under the Snyder's label in southwestern Pennsylvania. A court decided that each company had the right to Snyder's label. To avoid confusion, one Snyder's would label products Snyder's of Berlin and the other would use Snyder's of Hanover.

From the 1960s to the 1980s, Snyder's of Hanover developed a full line of pretzels, potato chips, cheese twists, popcorn, and tortilla chips.

In 1981, Snyder's of Hanover broke away from the Hanover Foods Corporation. Since then, Snyder's of Hanover, under the leadership of Michael Warehime, has continued its tradition of success.

The products made at Snyder's 300,000-square-foot York Street plant and its sister plant in Goodyear, Arizona, are shipped just about everywhere: North and South America, Europe, the Middle East, Asia, Pacific Rim countries, and to American military personnel around the world. Just reading about the extent of Snyder's distribution network boggles the mind. They have everything covered, from store delivery systems for the eastern United States to an independent distributor network for rest of the country, to a vending distributor network, food service distributors, an export division, and a mail-order catalog, not to mention corporate gift-giving and fund-raising options.

Snyder's of Hanover shows no signs of slowing down. In order to better serve its worldwide market, company owner Michael Warehime is considering the possibility of building a plant in Bastogne, Belgium, and another facility west of Chicago. In the snack food empire, Snyder's of Hanover is royalty.

The Tour

After you check in at the retail counter, you'll be directed upstairs to a room with several rows of chairs. Your guide will introduce you to the company, wowing you with numbers like these: This facility has seven ovens, each more than 150 feet long, one of which produces more than a ton of pretzels per hour. Snyder's uses more than 600,000 pounds of masa (corn flour) per month to make tortilla chips. Snyder's can ship three hundred thousand cases—that's two hundred trailer loads—of products per week. Three production shifts work around the clock seven days a week, shutting down only for maintenance and national holidays.

A seven-minute video gives you a feel for what you'll see on your tour. The video has no soundtrack, which gives the guide the opportunity to narrate and to answer questions as the film rolls. Don't expect to see how Snyder's of Hanover makes its special pretzels, though. The formula and the baking process are closely guarded secrets.

Pretzels are made two ways at Snyder's. One is by a pretzel-twisting machine. The video shows a neat close-up of this. A ball of dough is cut, rolled into a long noodle, and dropped into a wheel. "Fingers" on the machine mechanically twist the dough into a pretzel shape. This is how Snyder's makes its big, fat, hard pretzels.

The other manufacturing method is extrusion. Dough is forced through holes in a pretzel-shaped die, sliced to just the right thickness. An extruder makes twenty-four pretzels a stroke and runs at seventy-two strokes per minute—that's 1,728 pretzels per minute per machine.

Regular-thickness pretzels proof, or rise, on a belt. They're dipped into a heated bath of sodium hydroxide and water to give them that nice brown

Visiting Snyder's
HANOVER, PA

Mailing address: P.O. Box 917, Hanover, PA 17331

Fax number: 717-632-7207

E-mail address: consumeraffairs@snyders-han.com

Tour hours: Tuesday–Thursday, 10 A.M.–2 P.M. year-round. The factory store is open Monday–Saturday, 9 A.M.–6 P.M., and Sunday, noon–5 P.M. Closed major holidays.

Admission: Free.

Reservations: Required, at least twenty-four hours in advance.

Special considerations: The factory outlet store is wheelchair accessible, but the tour is not. No age restrictions. Strollers permitted, but you have to carry it up a flight of steps. No photographs permitted.

Tour length and type: About 1 hour. Guided tour begins with live introduction and videotape, then moves through galleries overlooking factory floor.

Group size: Maximum of forty people; larger groups will be divided. Individuals and families welcome.

On-site facilities: Factory store, restrooms.

Nearby attractions: Contact the York County Convention and Visitors Bureau at 888-858-YORK or visit the website www.yorkpa.org for information about attractions, including the Agricultural Museum of York County, Harley-Davidson Motorcycle Final Assembly Plant and Museum, the Historical Society Museum/York County Heritage Trust, and the York Barbell Museum and Weightlifting Hall of Fame. Utz Quality Foods in Hanover, Wolfgang Candy Co. in York, and Martin's Potato Chips in Thomasville, also welcome visitors.

Directions: From Hanover, take PA Route 116 East (York Street) 4 miles. The factory is on the left just past the corporate headquarters building.

sheen, then they go through the oven. After baking, they go to a dryer to remove more moisture.

When the video ends, you follow the guide into the hallway, where windows give a good vantage point into the factory. Stick close to the guide; if the group starts to fan out, you may miss hearing some of the narrative.

One of the first things you see is the boxes from the packaging room being moved by an automatic palletizer. I felt like I was looking at a robot world. Things were being transported, and there wasn't a person in sight. It was impressive and eerie at the same time. The next hallway has windows on both sides, and you can see real people down below. Snyder's of Hanover still does a lot of hand packaging.

You go past the bucket scales, where products are weighed, then dropped into waiting bags. As you pass the ovens, your guide may explain that they were specially designed for Snyder's and can be opened so that people with vacuum hoses can clean them from end to end quickly and efficiently.

In another hallway, the vantage point overlooks the corn chip line on one side and the potato chip line on the other. Snyder's of Hanover doesn't take any chances with raw materials: They contract for specific crops of potatoes three years in advance. It's fun to watch the spuds get washed, peeled, and sliced. Blades are changed once every shift to keep them razor sharp.

Work your way back along the gallery windows to where the tour began, and your group is likely to burst into applause—partly for the guide, who has given generously of knowledge and time, and partly for Snyder's of Hanover.

Sturgis Pretzel House

219 East Main Street
Lititz, PA 17543
717-626-4354
www.sturgispretzel.com

Lititz is home to the most venerable spot in American pretzel history: Sturgis Pretzel House. It was here, in the gracious stone home built by Er Bauet Von Peterkreiter in 1784, that Julius Sturgis got his mid-nineteenth-century start in what would become the country's first commercial pretzel bakery. You can follow in Sturgis's footsteps, learning how pretzels are made, watching them bake in the old oven, even twisting your own hunk of dough into a pretzel.

Legend has it that way back in 1850, breadmaker Julius Sturgis had some loaves cooking in the oven. A hobo hopped off a train about a half block away and followed the delicious aroma to the Sturgis house. He asked for some food and a job. Sturgis couldn't help him with the job, but he did invite the man to stay for dinner. To thank his host for the hospitality, the guest gave Sturgis a recipe for pretzels.

Sturgis was a skilled bread baker, but he had never made pretzels. He thought he'd give it a try, with his wife and their fourteen children as taste-testers. The pretzels were a big hit, so Sturgis added them to his product line. Eleven years later, in 1861, the pretzels had become so popular that Sturgis ditched the bread baking entirely and went into the pretzel-baking business full-time.

Today, the bakery is owned by Clyde and Barbara Ann Tshudy, who continue this pretzel-baking tradition. Clyde Tshudy, in fact, learned the pretzel trade from Lewis B. Sturgis, Julius's son. The Tshudys are credited with designing and baking a unique horse-and-buggy pretzel, the perfect shape to represent their Amish country location. Soft pretzels are still baked the old-fashioned way, but the Tshudys installed automated equipment in 1971 to handle a large volume of hard pretzels. One machine can extrude 245 pretzels in a minute, or 2 tons of hard pretzels in a day, compared with the hand-twisting record of 40 pretzels per minute.

Sturgis Pretzel House bakes and sells more than two dozen flavors, with and without salt. Traditionalists might opt for the old-fashioned or

*The big pretzel hangs outside America's first commercial
pretzel bakery.*

whole-wheat variety, while more adventurous types can try pretzels flavored with jalapeño or Maryland crab. If you like mustard on your pretzels but don't want the mess, try the honey mustard and onion variety.

Julius Sturgis would no doubt be proud at the recognition his enter-
prise still receives today. Sturgis Pretzel House has been featured on the
Food Network, in *U.S. News and World Report,* and in countless travel articles. Even the United States Department of the Interior has recognized its
significance: The property is listed on the National Register of Historic
Places. As far as pretzels go, this is hallowed ground.

The Tour

You know you're in the right place when you see the giant pretzel sign hanging outside the front door on Main Street in Lititz. Enter the building and go into the first room on your left to check in for the tour. The ticket is a pretzel: This tour is going to be fun.

Everyone moves through the next room and into the bakery area, where the tour guide invites people to find a space around a large, L-shaped counter. You can feel the heat of the oven as the guide distributes fist-size balls of dough. Pay attention: You're about to learn the fine art of pretzel twisting, and some pretzel lore, too.

When you've rolled your dough long and thin, the guide asks you to bend it into a U-shape, to signify prayers going up to heaven. Crossing the tops over makes an X, emblematic of tying the knot in marriage. Flip that X down and you've got a pretzel, more or less. Your efforts are rewarded with an Official Pretzel Twister's Certificate.

The tour continues in the next room, where another guide shows you how the baking process is done. Dough made from Lancaster County white winter wheat is rolled on a slatted wood surface. The wood provides resistance, while the spaces help keep it from sticking. The shaped dough is dipped into a solution of baking soda and water to give the pretzels that shiny brown finish. Pretzels are baked for ten minutes in a 550-degree oven.

Sturgis Pretzel House makes 3 million soft pretzels each year, and you're about to eat one of them. While you snack, you can shop in the combination pretzel, gift, and antique shop.

Occasionally, tours are taken to see the automated manufacturing facility, where 400 pounds of pretzels

Visitors learn to twist their own pretzels.

Visiting Sturgis Pretzel House

LITITZ, PA

Fax number: 717-627-2682

E-mail address:
info@sturgispretzel.com

Tour hours: Monday–Saturday,
9 A.M.–5 P.M. year-round. Last
tour starts at 4:30 P.M.

Admission: $2 per person; free
for children under two.

Reservations: Groups should call ahead;
others may want to call to find out how
full the tour schedule is for a particular
date and time.

Special considerations: Tour is wheelchair accessible but restrooms are
not. No age restrictions. Strollers
permitted. Still and video cameras
may be used, as long as the pictures
are for personal (noncommercial,
nonpublished) use only. Most
groups take their tours early in the
day. Individuals and families may
be asked to join a group. If you
prefer not to, phone ahead or check
in with the attendant and sign up
for a tour during a less-crowded
time of day. While you wait, stroll
the quaint streets of Lititz; it's a
delightful town.

Tour length and type: 25-minute
guided tour. Opportunity for
hands-on pretzel twisting.

Group size: Maximum of sixty people.
Individuals and families welcome.

On-site facilities: Factory/gift/antique
shop, restrooms, small picnic area.

Nearby attractions: Contact the Pennsylvania Dutch Convention and Visitors Bureau at 800-PA-DUTCH or visit
the website www.padutchcountry.com
for information about Lancaster-area
attractions, including Dutch Wonderland family amusement park, Ephrata
Cloister, factory outlets, James
Buchanan's Wheatland, Landis Valley
Museum, National Watch and Clock
Museum, Railroad Museum of Pennsylvania, Strasburg Railroad Company, wineries, and more. The Cake
And Kandy Emporium and Wilbur
Chocolate Candy Americana Museum
& Store, both in Lititz, also welcome
visitors, as do the Intercourse Canning
Company and the Intercourse Pretzel
Factory, in nearby Intercourse.

In Lititz, the Lititz Historical Foundation offers a brochure outlining
a self-guided walking tour. Pick one
up at the Johannes Mueller House,
137–139 East Main Street. Lititz
Springs Park is a nice spot to relax;
the visitors center is at the park's entrance. Kready's Country Store Museum is an original 1860s country
store that's open to visitors. Pick up
brochures at any attraction.

Directions: From the intersection of
U.S. Route 30 and PA Route 772 in
Gap, take Route 772 West to Lititz.
This becomes East Main Street. Stur-
gis Pretzel House is on the right. If
you come to a T, you've gone too far.

Or, from PA Route 501 and U.S.
Route 30, go north on 501 about 10
minutes. Turn right onto Main Street
in Lititz. Sturgis Pretzel House is on
the left.

are produced each hour. If you have that opportunity, be prepared for the heat radiating from ovens set at 500 degrees. Here you can see the extruded pretzels proofing on a conveyor, being coated with flavoring, and moving through the drying area.

The only difference between soft pretzels and hard ones is the moisture level. Hard pretzels are made by machine, with the dough forced through an extruder. It works kind of like the Play-Doh Fun Factory you may have had as a kid. After baking, the pretzels are spread on trays, where they dry out for several hours in 120-degree heat. The lack of moisture allows hard pretzels to stay fresh for months.

Michael Tshudy, president of Sturgis Pretzel House, explains the importance of tourism to his company. "Our major business is done right here, and through mail order," he says. Last year, more than forty-five thousand visitors toured the site where the American pretzel industry was born. Follow in their footsteps, and you'll agree that Sturgis Pretzel House is indeed "family fun with a twist."

CHOCOLATE AND CANDY

Without the cacao plant, there would be no chocolate. The tree was native to the rain forests of Central and South America and was domesticated around 400 B.C. by the Maya, who harvested its football-shaped, purplish-yellow pods. The Aztecs believed that the god Quetzalcoatl brought the tree with him from paradise and taught his people how to roast and grind the seeds, making a nourishing paste that could be dissolved in water. They consumed chocolate only as a beverage, called xocolatl (SHOCK-o-lattle). Both xocolatl and cacao were ritually significant to these early peoples. For example, as part of twelfth-century Mesoamerican marriages, the bride and groom shared a mug of frothy chocolate.

Christopher Columbus brought chocolate to Spain when he returned from his fourth voyage to the New World in 1502, but it was not given much attention. It wasn't until 1528, when Hernando Cortes brought the Aztec recipe for xocolatl from Mexico to Spain's Charles V, that chocolate was considered important. Cortes described chocolate as "the divine drink, which builds up resistance and fights fatigue. A cup of this precious drink permits a man to walk for a whole day without food."

The Spaniards kept chocolate-making methods secret for almost a century. Monks in Spanish monasteries processed the beans. As the stimulating drink with sugar, vanilla, and cinnamon became popular on the continent, this proprietary knowledge was profitable for Spain, which planted cacao trees in its tropical colonies.

As Spain's power declined, the secret of cacao was revealed to the rest of Europe. In France, chocolate was at first considered a "barbarous product and noxious drug." Chocolate's future was ensured, however, when French queen Anne of Austria, wife of Louis XIII, declared chocolate as the drink of the French court in 1615.

Opposite: Hand clustering at Asher's/Lewistown.

A Chocolate Glossary

Bittersweet chocolate. See *Semisweet chocolate.*

Bloom. The whitish haze that forms on chocolate when cocoa butter has been exposed to temperature fluctuations. You may have seen bloom on chocolate that was stored in the refrigerator. Despite its looks, it is safe to eat.

Cacao. The product of the cacao plant, as well as the plant itself.

Chocolate liquor. Produced when the cocoa bean nib is finely ground to a smooth liquid state. (It is liquid when warm, solid when cooled.) The chocolate liquor can then be cooled and molded into blocks also known as unsweetened baking chocolate. The liquor and blocks contain roughly 53 percent cocoa butter. They contain no alcohol.

Cocoa, or cocoa powder. The solid that remains after the cocoa butter is pressed out of chocolate liquor.

Cocoa butter. The vegetable fat present in cocoa beans. It is released when the chocolate liquor is pressed. It is solid at room temperature but melts in the mouth at body temperature.

Cocoa powder. See *cocoa.*

Conching. The process in which heavy rollers move liquid chocolate back and forth, kneading it to make it smooth.

Around the mid-1650s, chocolate became the rage. Chocolate shops sprang up by the dozens. Only the elite could afford to indulge, though, especially when England imposed a hefty duty on chocolate.

In the United States, chocolate was first manufactured in 1765. It was introduced at Milton Lower Mills, near Dorchester, Massachusetts, by John Hanan, who brought cocoa beans from the West Indies, thinking they might be used in medicine. He got together with physician James Baker, and they started the first chocolate factory in North America, where they made cures, not candy.

The invention of the cocoa press in 1828 by C. J. Van Houten, a Dutch chocolate maker, helped reduce the price and make chocolate

Confectionery coating, or summer coating. A blend of sugar, milk powder, hardened vegetable oil, and flavoring used as a dip for candies. It comes in a variety of pastel colors. Some coatings have low-fat cocoa powder added, but none contain cocoa butter or can be classified as chocolate.

Couverture. Professional-quality coating chocolate that is extremely glossy. Couverture melts smoothly but requires tempering. It usually contains a minimum of 32 percent cocoa butter, which enables it to form a much thinner shell than ordinary confectionery coating. Couverture is usually found only in specialty candy-making shops, where it is used to surround chocolate-covered fruits or as the shell of fancy filled chocolates.

Dark chocolate. See *Semisweet chocolate.*

Dutch process cocoa. Made by adding alkali to nibs or cocoa powder to develop flavor, reduce acidity, and make it more soluble. This also darkens the color.

Ganache. A thick, extremely rich chocolate spread, often used between the layers of gourmet chocolate cakes. Ganache is made by pouring hot cream over chopped up chocolate and whipping the mixture until the chocolate melts and it becomes thick and stiff.

(continued on page 50)

available to the masses. Squeezing out the cocoa butter from the beans also removed the acidity and bitterness.

In the mid-1860s, Daniel Peter of Switzerland attempted to add milk to chocolate to make it smoother. After eight years of experimentation, Peter took his problem to Henry Nestlé, who had perfected the manufacture of condensed milk. Nestlé and Peter mixed sweetened condensed milk with chocolate, and milk chocolate was born.

Rodolphe Lindt of Bern, Switzerland, invented a refining technique called conching in 1879. Lindt also added some cocoa butter back into the chocolate, which helped it firm up into a bar and allowed it to melt on the tongue.

A Chocolate Glossary

(continued from page 49)

Liquid chocolate. Unsweetened chocolate that is made with vegetable oil rather than cocoa butter, so it does not have the same texture or flavor as regular unsweetened chocolate. It is convenient to use in baking because it requires no melting.

Milk chocolate. Sweetened chocolate with whole and/or skim milk added. It consists of cocoa butter, milk, sweeteners, and flavorings added to chocolate liquor. Milk chocolate is good for garnishes and candy coatings. All milk chocolate made in the United States must contain at least 10 percent chocolate liquor and 12 percent whole milk.

Nibs. The center, or meat, of the cocoa bean.

Semisweet chocolate. Also called dark chocolate or bittersweet chocolate, this is chocolate liquor with additional sweeteners and cocoa butter. According to U.S. standards, it must contain at least 35 percent chocolate liquor. It also contains added cocoa butter, sugar, vanilla or vanillin, and often lecithin, a soy-based emulsifier. Its fat content averages 27 percent.

Summer coating. See *Confectionery coating.*

In 1894, Milton S. Hershey established the Hershey Chocolate Company in Pennsylvania, paving the way for the love affair between Americans and chocolate that continues to this day. Our average annual chocolate consumption is about 11.5 pounds per person. And when it comes to chocolate production, Pennsylvania is number one in the nation.

The more than sixty chocolate candy manufacturers in Pennsylvania cranked out shipments of product worth more than $1.6 billion in 1997, the most recent year for which the U.S. Census Bureau has statistics available. Of all the chocolate made in the United States, Pennsylvania produces more than 38 percent.

Part of the reason is the presence of Hershey Foods Corporation, whose 1999 sales were close to $4 billion. But that's only a piece of the

Sweet chocolate. Made by mixing and grinding chocolate liquor with one or more nutritive carbohydrate sweeteners. It contains at least 15 percent chocolate liquor. Sweet chocolate is used mostly for decorating and garnishing. Its fat content is similar to that of semisweet chocolate.

Tempering. The process of turning melted chocolate into a solid mass of stable cocoa butter crystals with fine, even-grained texture by the controlled heating and cooling of the chocolate with agitation. This allows fine-grained, aligned crystals to form, instead of less stable and more random crystals.

Theobroma cacao. The botanical name for cacao. The genus name, *Theobroma,* is derived from the Greek words for "god" and "food."

Unsweetened chocolate. Also called baking chocolate or bitter chocolate. U.S. standards require that unsweetened chocolate contain between 50 and 58 percent cocoa butter.

White chocolate. Contains sugar, cocoa butter, milk solids, and flavorings such as vanilla. It does not contain chocolate liquor or nonfat cocoa solids. White chocolate is often used as a coating and is the most fragile form of chocolate. Imitation white chocolate is made with vegetable oil rather than cocoa butter.

story. Small, medium-size, and large candy companies across the state also contribute.

You can see a wide range in automation and manufacturing styles at the factories that welcome visitors, from highly robotic production to old-style hand-dipping methods. Consistent across the board, though, are the quality of Pennsylvania-made chocolates and the dedication of the candy makers.

My favorite among the state's candies is the dark-chocolate-covered pretzel. What could be more quintessentially Pennsylvania? If you sample nothing else, give one of these a try. The smooth, semisweet chocolate is an especially good combination with the crunchiness and saltiness of the pretzel. Ask the tour guide what specialties he or she recommends, and take home a bag when you finish your visit. You won't be disappointed.

Asher's Chocolates

80 Wambold Road
Souderton, PA 18964
215-721-3276 or 800-438-8882
www.ashers.com

The smell of sugar outside the pretty red and white building is the first thing you notice at the headquarters of Asher's Chocolates, the oldest family owned and operated candy manufacturer in the country. Just about everyone knows the Asher's name, and it's no wonder: Asher's has been making fine chocolates and candy confections since 1892. With more than half of the company's 6 million pounds of annual output packaged under private labels, chances are you've eaten plenty of delicious Asher's candy without even realizing it.

Chester A. Asher emigrated from Canada in 1890 and founded the business two years later. His first factory was in center city Philadelphia. In 1898, the firm relocated to the Germantown section of the city. Asher's Chocolates remained in Germantown for more than nine decades, expanding over the years to occupy several buildings. In 1998, the company moved its factory, shipping, and offices to a new 125,000-square-foot facility in Souderton. The facility's design permits efficient work flow, from receiving through processing to shipping.

Chester A. Asher's four sons ran the company until 1966, when third-generation Ashers John L. Jr. and Robert took over. They were later joined by David B. and Jeffrey S., members of the fourth Asher generation. Under the direction of these third- and fourth-generation representatives, Asher's Chocolates continues the tradition of quality and purity that began more than a century ago.

The Tour

Tours begin in the attractive retail space that's designed to look like a Victorian candy store. Check in at the counter, and you are directed up a ramp, past photographs of the founder and other family members.

The viewing area is a long hallway with glass on one side and beautiful hand-painted murals on the other. Turn to the left as soon as you get to the hallway, then walk all the way to the end. The murals present a history of the company in vivid pictorial detail, as well as an explanation of how cacao beans become chocolate. Read them as you move down the hall, and you're ready to start the multimedia tour that explains what you're seeing on the factory floor below.

Activate the first video monitor—there are four in all—and you'll learn some basic facts about Asher's Chocolates and the state-of-the-art factory you're visiting. Fresh ingredients such as sugar, corn syrup, honey, cream, and chocolate are delivered to the receiving area, where they are thoroughly inspected. Next, candy centers and other items are prepared in the kitchens. In the fudge kitchen, the raw materials are blended and heated in gleaming copper or stainless steel kettles. Toffee is also rolled and cut in the kitchen area.

Now the video presentation explains the fascinating machine you see right in front of you. It's a Mogul machine, which stamps shapes into cornstarch, thereby creating temporary molds. Trays of these molds are transported on boards, and confection is deposited in them. The trays are placed on pallets to let the candy cool. Then the machine turns the trays upside down above a wire mesh belt to dump out the finished centers. A blast of air removes any remaining starch.

Another method that Asher's uses to make candy centers is extrusion. Ingredients are mixed into a thick paste. The extruder forces the

The candies come down the line for packaging.

Different kinds of candies are boxed in assortments.

sweet goo through holes in metal dies, and a knife cuts them off at intervals to get the right-size pieces.

The next monitor starts off with an explanation of the enrobing process. Numbers posted above different stations in the factory correspond to what the voice on the video is explaining. First, chocolate washes underneath the centers. That's called bottoming. The centers then sashay through a curtain of tempered chocolate and a second bottomer bath before heading for the cooling tunnel.

Some of the other action down on the floor takes place on the specialty toffee line, where Asher's popular buttercrunch is made. This process requires a skilled candy maker to cook the ingredients over a gas fire at high temperature, spread the mixture on a metal table to cool, and score it just right. After the candy sets, it's broken up by hand, enrobed in chocolate, and coated with nuts.

You also see nonpareils pass through a bed of sugar beads known as seeds, whole nuts being mixed with tempered chocolate to form almond bark, a sugar-free extrusion line, and more. Clustering is automated here on specialty production lines, which mix solid ingredients like coconut or other nuts with tempered chocolate to form a paste that's deposited

Visiting Asher's Chocolates

SOUDERTON, PA

Fax number: 215-721-3209

E-mail address: Tours@ashers.com

Tour hours: Monday–Friday, 9:30 A.M.–3:00 P.M. year-round; Saturday call for hours, no regular schedule. Closed Sundays and holidays. It is recommended that you start any weekday tour by 2:30 P.M.

Admission: Free.

Reservations: Required for groups of ten or more.

Special considerations: Wheelchair accessible. No age restrictions. Strollers permitted. Still and video cameras permitted.

Tour length and type: About 25 minutes. Self-guided video tour with views of the factory floor; tour guide available on request for large groups.

Group size: Maximum of thirty people, (twenty-five or less recommended). Individuals and families welcome.

On-site facilities: Candy store and gift shop, restrooms.

Special events: Fall festival, one Saturday in mid-October, with fire engines, live music, costumed characters, and candy. Call for details.

Nearby attractions: Contact the Valley Forge Convention and Visitors Bureau at 888-VISIT-VF or visit the website www.valleyforge.org for information about Montgomery County attractions. Since Souderton is close to the Bucks County border, you may also want to contact the Bucks County Conference and Visitors Bureau at 800-836-BUCKS or visit www.buckscountycvb.org. Some attractions include Graeme Park, Hope Lodge, Mercer and Fonthill Museums, Mill Grove/Audubon Wildlife Sanctuary, Moravian Pottery and Tile Works, Peddler's Village, Skippack Village, and Valley Forge National Historical Park.

Directions: From the Lansdale Exit, Exit 31 of the Northeast Extension of the PA Turnpike, turn right onto PA Route 63 (Sumneytown Pike). Turn right again onto Wambold Road. Asher's Chocolates is ahead on the left in approximately 1 mile.

on conveyors by machine. Another enrobing line is devoted to white chocolate confections.

With so much candy going to so many destinations, impeccable quality control is essential. Asher's has its own quality assurance laboratory. Employees armed with microscopes perform rigorous and frequent inspections on everything from raw materials to the products that come off each line as processing occurs. Molds are thoroughly washed, rinsed with deionized water, and dried.

At the third monitor, you learn something about the tempering process—how temperature and humidity are controlled to produce that glossy look of fine chocolate. Coolers blow air over the candy in three zones. First comes a soft breeze of 65-degree air. Next, the air blows harder and cooler, at 55 degrees. In the third zone, the candy is re-warmed to 65 degrees. This avoids the formation of moisture on the surface of the chocolate.

The molding area of the factory isn't visible from the gallery, but you can see some of it done on the screen. You also see the clever way that Asher's makes chocolate-covered cherries. Liquid chocolate is piped into molds, then cooled just long enough for the outside to set, kind of like what happens when you empty an ice tray before the water is completely frozen. The chocolate "skin" is cooled gently to set the shell, then it's passed under a depositor that adds the cherry and the sweet surround. More chocolate is poured on; this will be the bottom of the candy after it's cooled and demolded. Cordials are foil-wrapped for looks and protection.

Video four shows the packing process. After the candy is passed through metal detectors, it's packed by hand, then stored in a climate-controlled warehouse that can hold a million pounds of candy. Strict stock rotation ensures maximum freshness for the more than two hundred types of candy that will be sent to all fifty states and abroad.

After the final video, you may want to look at the table display about chocolate production. Samples of beans, nibs, cocoa cake, chocolate liquor, cocoa butter, and dark and milk chocolate give a good overview of how the unassuming cacao bean is turned into heavenly treats.

Back in the old-fashioned candy store, pick up a fresh candy sample, then shop to your heart's content. With some gentle prodding from the counter personnel, I finally took the plunge and tried my first chocolate-covered potato chip. Surprise: I liked it a lot! A small, semienclosed area with a little table, chairs, and a tea set is very appealing to the younger set. Kids love to have pretend tea parties with the resident teddy bears. It's that kind of friendly atmosphere that makes Asher's Chocolates—as big and successful as it is—feel like family.

Asher's Chocolates/Lewistown (formerly Goss Candies)

19 East Susquehanna Avenue
Lewistown, PA 17044
717-248-8613

Until its acquisition by Asher's in 1991, Goss Candies was a small firm. Now, along with its bigger partner, the renamed Asher's/Lewistown is a thriving, growing company that has introduced technological improvements where it makes sense, while still making many products by hand, using original recipes. You get the feeling of both tradition and optimism at Asher's/Lewistown, where the extensive factory tour showcases old-fashioned and modern methods of candy making.

Harry Goss and his family founded Goss Candies in 1913, at the corner of Logan and Spruce Streets in Lewistown. Maximum output was a few pounds of sweets per day. The company has moved three times since then: to 317 Valley Street in 1921, to 500 Valley Street twenty years later, then in 1997 to its present location at 19 East Susquehanna Avenue. Interestingly, the move from 317 to 500 Valley Street in June 1941 was a swap in which the City Hook and Ladder Company and Goss Candy Company changed places.

Goss Candies also changed ownership over the years. After Harry Goss, the company was purchased in turn by the Stoner, Madiero, and Hershey families (unrelated to the famous Hershey of chocolates), and then by Asher's Chocolates. The product line changed, too, from retail to wholesale to specialty products.

The company has given a lot to the community. Along with its high-quality products, Asher's/Lewistown contributes to the local tax base, buys local products whenever possible, uses local businesses to do adjunct work, raises funds for the area, and offers employment. Today, Asher's/Lewistown has a workforce of seventy.

Technological improvements include new packaging and sealing machines, melters, and a tempering machine to track the condition of the chocolate. Nutritional analyses and labeling has been a large investment for Asher's/Lewistown. The chocolate from the suppliers has been improved to be resistant to bloom, the white coating that chocolate develops when it gets too cold. And new ingredients have made sugar-free chocolate tastier and easier to work with.

Since the Asher family bought the company in 1991, business has increased greatly. Production rose from 40,000 pounds of candy a year to over 1 million pounds annually, and continued growth is forecast.

The Tour

Your first encounter with Asher's/Lewistown is in its large retail space, where wood-and-glass cases and skirted tables showcase candy items, from molded chocolate pigs to a spectacular white chocolate Cinderella coach pulled by six horses. Penn State merchandise confirms that you're in Nittany Lion country. Chocolate long-stemmed roses are a tasty Valentine's Day alternative to the petal-dropping kind.

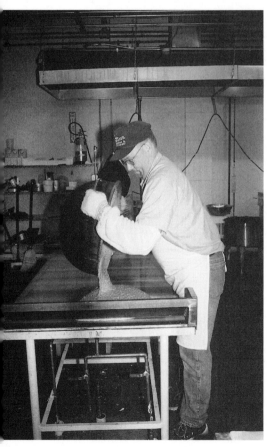

Pouring almond buttercrunch.

The real fun begins when your tour guide escorts you into the factory. My guide, assistant manager Judy Folk, was knowledgeable and well informed, friendly yet low-key. She explained that Asher's/Lewistown uses Nestlé chocolate, which arrives in 1,500-pound skids. Wilbur supplies the factory with peanut butter bits and sugar-free chocolate. Nuts—pecans, almonds, cashews, peanuts, pistachios, and walnuts—are stored in a special room with controlled humidity and temperature.

The day I visited, three flavors of saltwater taffy were hardening. They were destined to be coated in dark chocolate, wrapped in foil, and sold by companies at the shore that I thought made their own products. The man supervising the hardening process cut a

A bar smooths almond buttercrunch to a uniform thickness.

piece of orange-flavored taffy for me, just one of the many samples I was offered on my tour.

Almond buttercrunch is one of the company's most popular products, so it's cooked every day. It's also a wonderful example of hands-on candy making. The crunch maker greases a table as the hot mixture bubbles in a copper kettle. When table and mixture are ready, he dons thick gloves, lifts the kettle off the heat, and expertly pours the molten crunch onto the table, leaving exactly the right margin between the candy and the table's edge. A bar runs over the candy to smooth it to uniform thickness, then it is scored and left to cool. Another batch is begun, and the process continues.

The enrobing area is fun, too. You might see nuts being double-coated, to ensure that their oils are kept inside, or candied orange peel going over the "bottomer" and then through the chocolate waterfall. Coated confections go through cooling tunnels until they release easily from the conveyor belts.

Buttercrunch has ground almonds squeezed onto it by hand. Don't be put off by the lack of rubber gloves. Judy Folk explains: "You can't feel the temperature and texture of the candy with gloves, and gloves can get

Visiting Asher's/Lewistown

LEWISTOWN, PA

Fax number: 717-248-8637

Tour hours: Monday–Friday, 8:30 A.M.–3:30 P.M. year-round. (The last tour starts at 2:30 P.M.) The store is open Monday–Saturday, 8:30 A.M.–5 P.M.

Admission: Free.

Reservations: Required. Call several weeks in advance.

Special considerations: Wheelchair accessible. No age restrictions. Strollers permitted. Some photography is permitted upon request. The tour goes through a working factory. Wear closed-toed, nonskid shoes.

Tour length and type: A little more than an hour. Guided tour of the factory floor.

Group size: Maximum of twenty-five people. Will split large groups or combine small groups if necessary. Individuals and families welcome.

On-site facilities: Retail shop, restrooms.

Nearby attractions: Contact the Juniata-Mifflin Counties Tourist Promotion Agency at 877-568-9739 or visit the website www.juniatavalley.org for information about scenic and cultural attractions in and around Lewistown, including the Lewistown Narrows, Penn's Cave, the Pennsylvania Military Museum, Pennsylvania State University, and the Seven Mountain District.

Directions: Going west toward Lewistown on U.S. Route 322 from Harrisburg, there will be a split between 322 and U.S. Route 522. Take 522/22 straight onto South Main Street. In four blocks, turn right at Lake Chevrolet. Asher's/Lewistown is located across the street, behind the UniMart.

just as dirty as hands. We have strict hand-washing procedures here. There is a Clorox wash and nail brushes in every bathroom."

Asher's/Lewistown has invested in a nifty machine called a Doboy (pronounced "dough boy"). It takes a filled bag and seals it, then puts on the header—the label across the top—and punches a hole from which to hang the bag.

The company makes a lot of private-label items, so you may find Asher's/Lewistown candy in some surprising locations. The Mickey Mouse–shaped chocolates at Disney World are Asher's/Lewistown products, as are nonpareils and coated pretzels at Veterans Stadium in Philadelphia, candy at the MGM Grand in Las Vegas, chocolates sold by Boscov's, and even some items sold under the Hershey's label.

In the clustering area, workers dip fingerfuls of coconut or other centers into melted chocolate, placing the coated results precisely on trays. These are transported to the refrigerator room to harden. A shiny coating results because the chocolate has been perfectly tempered.

The chocolate-molding department is busy, especially during the Christmas and Easter seasons. It's not unusual for Asher's/Lewistown to make more than two hundred thousand molded items for the Easter season. Every piece of molded chocolate is hand trimmed, then carefully wrapped in tissue paper until it's time to seal it up.

Here, as is the case throughout the factory, the employees work steadily but not frantically. They are happy to answer questions, smile at visitors, and offer a sample of whatever they're working on. It's refreshing that in a factory that produces more than a million pounds of candy per year, personal touches like that haven't disappeared.

Cake And Kandy Emporium

53 East Main Street (rear)
Lititz, PA 17543-1902
717-625-4646

CAKE AND KANDY EMPORIUM

Sometimes traditions die out quietly, passing into extinction without anyone noticing. But sometimes, before it's too late, someone with a passion sees the value in the old ways and takes up the cause. One such preservationist is Nancy Fasolt, who has single-handedly breathed new life into the Pennsylvania Dutch Christmas tradition of clear toy candy. Thanks to her efforts, a custom that has been traced back to the mid-1800s is alive and well in the twenty-first century.

Christmas was simple and spiritual for the Pennsylvania Dutch, without the overwhelming materialism we often see today. "Children would set their plates on Christmas Eve," says Fasolt. "The next morning they would find nuts, an apple or an orange, and clear toy candy, shaped like animals or other toys. Those were the only toys they'd get for Christmas. The children would play with the clear toy candy until they couldn't wait any longer, then they'd wash it off and eat it."

Because of the way light gleams through the translucent candy, some people also used clear toy candy for tree ornaments. One old legend recounts that in a Philadelphia carnival side show "glass-eating" act, the "glass" that the man chewed and swallowed was actually clear toy candy.

Fasolt explains the essentials of clear toy candy. "The candy has only three ingredients: water, sugar, and corn syrup," she says. "Traditionally, the candy is yellow—which is the natural color of the syrup—or red or green. Food coloring is used to make those two colors."

Hard candy and clear toy candy are not the same, although Fasolt didn't know this at first. A key difference is that hard candy has flavoring added; clear toy candy doesn't. Fasolt had been making clear toy candy the wrong way until Celie Malone, who had owned Celie's Sweet Shop in Lancaster in the 1940s, visited Fasolt's shop. In her eighties, Malone took one look at a piece of clear toy candy and said with skepticism, "You teach classes in this?" When Fasolt responded in the affirmative, Malone shook her head and said, "Someday I'm going to teach you how to make clear toy candy!"

Malone was as good as her word, and the two spent many hours together. Fasolt used the opportunity to hone her skills and to learn more about clear toy candy.

Another result of these lessons was Fasolt's growing interest in antique candy molds. The molds come in all kinds of animal and toy shapes, from rabbits and camels to trains and tea sets. Most molds were made by two Philadelphia companies, Thomas Mills Brothers and V. Clad Company. About 425 patterns were produced by Mills, ranging in size from 1 to more than 6 1/2 inches tall.

Nancy Fasolt and her daughter pour clear toy candy. COURTESY OF NANCY FASOLT

Pattern molds were fashioned in yellow brass. These brass molds were not used to make candy. Instead, food-use molds were produced from them. Molds produced in the Mills or V. Clad factories are marked as such. These originals are highly prized by collectors and, depending on their size, can fetch well over $100 apiece. Fasolt uses original molds, as well as some copies for her clear toys; they have been tested to ensure that they're food safe. Heavy and smooth, the molds are beautifully intricate. One of Fasolt's favorites is a stag, unusual because it comes in three pieces: two pieces that make up the animal, plus a third piece that forms the antlers and serves as a stand to hold the mold in position when it's filled.

The Cake And Kandy Emporium makes a full line of delectable edibles, but when autumn comes, everything else takes a backseat to the clear toy candy. "Starting in October, the whole place turns into clear toy heaven," says the candy maker. "We have seven or eight people working. We have to have somebody to cook, somebody to pour, someone to unmold. Plus, each piece has to be trimmed by hand. We start at seven in the morning and work until four or five."

Using 4-quart pots on a two-burner stove, Fasolt and her helpers cook 3 pounds of mixture at a time, washing the pots between batches. The ingredients are heated to 300 degrees F. An accurate thermometer is essential for the success of the process.

While the syrup is cooking, the molds—up to three hundred at a time—are prepared. They're oiled with vegetable spray, then the halves are fastened together with rubber bands. Next, they're turned on their heads and lined up as close as possible, nestling together on two long tables near the stove. This arrangement minimizes the amount of mixture that drips during pouring. "Once you start pouring, you have to pour continuously," Fasolt says.

It takes strength, coordination, and experience to pour a thin stream without interruption until the pot is empty. During the busy season, Fasolt pours up to fifty pots daily, which yields close to three thousand pieces. All of the candy is trimmed and packed the same day it's made.

One advantage of the old molds over today's plastic and aluminum models is their ability to transfer heat quickly. "With the heavy molds, as soon as you finish pouring, you can start unmolding," Fasolt explains. The plastic molds can handle the heat fine, but it takes longer for the candy to cool. In addition, the life span of a plastic mold is about three years. "The old ones last forever," says Fasolt.

Weather also affects the speed at which the candy sets, as well as its clarity. "The colder and drier, the better," says Fasolt. "We have to open the doors to let cold air in when we're making clear toy. There's one mold, an elephant, that weighs 13 pounds. The finished elephant weighs more than 2 pounds. We have to do that one out on the porch." It can get pretty chilly out there, so Fasolt and her staff have to dress warmly.

Since clear toy candy was made to be played with, the old-fashioned versions didn't have lollipop sticks. Fasolt offers her candy both ways: the traditional, stickless candy and the more contemporary incarnation of

Nancy Fasolt with some of her clear toy candy creations.
COURTESY OF NANCY FASOLT

clear toy candy on a stick. Another change she's had to make is from olive oil to vegetable oil for greasing the molds. Modern American children, unused to the potent taste of olive oil, didn't like its flavor. Fasolt realized how important it was for kids to enjoy the candy. If they didn't go for it, they wouldn't pass the tradition on to their own children. So she switched to vegetable spray.

The sweet aroma of *Dierich Orde Glass,* as the Pennsylvania Dutch called it, permeates the shop throughout the fall. Your home can smell this way, too. Rather than keep the recipe and technique a closely guarded secret, Fasolt happily encourages others to make their own clear toy candy. She sells supplies, including a clear toy candy starter kit, and generously gives advice.

"I had to learn a lot about corn syrup," she says. "When you shop for corn syrup, you usually find Karo syrup, but that's not right for clear toy. You need a high-viscosity corn syrup that's almost like glucose. Another thing I learned is that not all corn syrup is made by the same process. One process makes corn syrup for marshmallow, which is the exact opposite of what we want for clear toy."

Anyone who gets serious about this hobby can purchase aluminum or plastic molds at the Cake And Kandy Emporium. Antique candy molds are also for sale. Fasolt cautions would-be candy makers that this hobby is not a children's activity. With a 300-degree molten mixture being handled, this cooking is for adults only. Fasolt welcomes visitors of all ages to watch clear toy candy being made in her shop but wants parents to know that for safety's sake, children must be well behaved.

Although she is best known for her clear toy candy, Nancy Fasolt is an accomplished artisan in other confectionery areas as well. It all started at Thanksgiving in 1982, when the Fasolts were visiting friends in Con-

Visiting Cake And Kandy Emporium

LITITZ, PA

E-mail address: cake@redrose.net

Tour hours: Clear toy candy is made Monday–Wednesday, 11 A.M.–4 P.M., from October–Christmas, weather permitting. Regular retail hours are Tuesday–Saturday, 10 A.M.–4 P.M. year-round. Candy making (other than clear toy) and cake decorating are on demand, so there are no scheduled production hours.

Admission: Free.

Reservations: Not necessary.

Special considerations: Wheelchair accessibility has been promised by landlord but is not installed yet. Well-behaved children are welcome. Strollers are not permitted. Still cameras okay; no video cameras.

Tour length and type: Explanation of the clear toy candy history and process by Nancy Fasolt and her helpers takes 5 to 10 minutes, but you may watch the candy-making process as long as you like.

Group size: Small groups only. About ten people can fit comfortably in the store at one time. Individuals and families welcome.

On-site facilities: Candy store only. No public restrooms.

Nearby attractions: Contact the Pennsylvania Dutch Convention and Visitors Bureau at 800-PA-DUTCH or visit the website www.padutchcountry.com for information about Lancaster-area attractions, including Dutch Wonderland family amusement park, Ephrata Cloister, factory outlets, James Buchanan's Wheatland, Landis Valley Museum, National Watch and Clock Museum, Railroad Museum of Pennsylvania, Strasburg Railroad Company, wineries, and more. Sturgis Pretzel House and Wilbur Chocolate Candy Americana Museum & Store, both in Lititz, also welcome visitors, as do the Intercourse Canning Company and the Intercourse Pretzel Factory, in nearby Intercourse.

In Lititz, the Lititz Historical Foundation offers a brochure outlining a self-guided walking tour. Pick one up at the Johannes Mueller House, 137–139 East Main Street. Lititz Springs Park is a nice spot to relax; the visitors center is at the park's entrance. Kready's Country Store Museum is an original 1860s country store that's open to visitors. Pick up brochures at any attraction.

Directions: From the intersection of U.S. Route 30 and PA Route 772 in Gap, take Route 772 West to Lititz. This becomes East Main Street. The Cake And Kandy Emporium is on the right, in the rear. If you come to a T, you've gone too far. To get to the parking lot behind the store, turn right into Sturgis Lane.

Or, from PA Route 501 and U.S. Route 30, take Route 501 North for about 10 minutes. Turn right onto Main Street in Lititz. The Emporium is on the left side in the rear. To get to the parking lot behind the store, turn left into Sturgis Lane.

necticut. "They had chocolate turkeys for dinner favors. I thought they were really neat, so I asked my friend how much they cost. When she told me, I was shocked. I thought, 'I can do that; they can't cost that much to make.'" Fasolt signed up for a candy-making class, and *voilà!* A career was launched.

Fasolt got into the cake-decorating field in much the same way, and with equally good results. A friend needed assistance making a wedding cake and talked Fasolt into helping. The next thing she knew, she was taking cake-decorating classes. Now, her wedding cakes rival anything Martha Stewart could whip up. The Cake And Kandy Emporium makes custom multitier cakes in English fondant and butter cream, embellished with Belgian lace drapes and bows, dotted with flowers of fondant or gum paste. The detail work is just gorgeous.

Cakes are just one example of Nancy Fasolt's natural flair and ceaseless curiosity about what she does and how to do it better. She's a member of the Canadian Society of Sugar Artistry, as well as the British Sugar-Craft Guild. Her first Emporium opened in 1985 at Fiddler's Green in Neffsville. In 1989, Fasolt moved the store to East Petersburg. She relocated to Lititz in October 1999.

The Cake And Kandy Emporium serves up bunnies, ducks, and hand-dipped eggs at Easter. Fasolt created a unique confection, chocolate quilt patches, that are perfect for visitors to take home from Pennsylvania Dutch Country. Traditional nine-patch, fan, and LeMoyne star quilt patterns are made of confectionery in assorted colors. Fasolt's truffles are also popular items. No matter what's being made, you can watch the candy makers at work.

It's not just the locals who recognize Fasolt's talent. Her chocolate creations make frequent appearances on the "Today Show," and in 1993, *Country Woman* magazine ran a feature on Fasolt and her clear toy candy. Recently, Fasolt's expertise with clear toy candy so impressed the Hershey Museum that she was invited to help equip the working kitchen in their Old Time Candy Kitchen exhibit with nineteenth-century tools. A replica of Milton Hershey's 1876 candy store on Spring Garden Street in Philadelphia, the exhibit includes a demonstration of clear toy candy making. Fasolt also presents her confections at the annual Pennsylvania State Farm Show. She is a member of Retail Confectioners International.

Nancy Fasolt's ancestors were among those who introduced clear toy candy to America. She remembers listening to her mother describe the joy of finding clear toy candy on her plate on Christmas Day, and she has fond memories of getting clear toy candy in her Christmas stocking. Thanks to her, others will have the opportunity to experience the same delight. Take home some clear toy candy and start your own family tradition.

Daffin's Candies

Main retail store and Chocolate Kingdom
496 East State Street
Sharon, PA 16146
724-342-2892 or 877-323-3465

Factory and retail store
7 Spearman Avenue
Farrell, PA 16121
724-983-8336

www.daffins.com

Forget those pip-squeak 6-ounce chocolate Easter bunnies you're used to; the Chocolate Kingdom boasts a whopper of a solid chocolate turtle that tips the scales at more than 400 pounds. His familiar and exotic animal buddies are equally impressive: a herd of deer, a family of elephants, even a rhinoceros.

It's not just chocolate animals that decorate this bedroom-size display behind a low picket fence: The architectural elements are also made of chocolate. Take a few minutes to marvel at the detail on the storybook castle, the miniature village, the clever train layout, and the Ferris wheel in the back. Somebody obviously had a lot of fun setting this up.

New layers of chocolate are added when the critters start to whiten and lose their shine, kind of like repointing a brick wall. While you're looking all this over, one of the staff members may pop by to offer you a sample piece of chocolate and answer questions.

The Chocolate Kingdom is at Daffin's State Street location, home of the self-proclaimed 15,000-square-foot "world's largest candy store." The factory tour is held at the company's second location in nearby Farrell.

Chocolate Kingdom was the brainchild of Paul "Pete" Daffin, grandson of the company's founder, George Daffin. Pete was a natural in the business who claimed that the first thing he ever smelled was chocolate. The original family store was started in 1903 by George in Woodsfield, Ohio. After World War I, George's son, Alec, moved the business to New Philadelphia, Ohio. Chocolate really started to sell during the 1920s,

Daffin's Candies's trademark: Peter Rabbit's giant chocolate castle. COURTESY OF DAFFIN'S CANDIES

thanks to the introduction of air-conditioning, which helped prevent melting and made it feasible for stores to offer the product year-round.

The company's next relocation took place in 1936, when Alec died. Pete and his mother, Georgia, moved the operations to Canton, Ohio.

Pete was sent to Europe courtesy of the U.S. Army during World War II. After he returned from duty, he decided to build his own candy factory and store in Sharon. The small downtown location opened in 1947, and the Daffin's reputation began to spread. A big boost to the business came when Pete and his wife, Jean, collaborated to create a solid chocolate Peter Rabbit for the Easter season. The bunny was a huge success, and demand for Daffin's candy soared. Things went so well that in 1975, the couple relocated their business to the 15,000-square-foot Sharon store. They also built a 30,000-square-foot factory in Farrell.

Since Pete Daffin's death in February 1998, the business has been run by Jean Daffin, president, and daughter Diane, vice president. Connie Leon, a longtime employee, is manager of all retail operations. Gary Sigler, a nephew, is general manager of the factory and manufacturing division. Other family members serve in various capacities at the store and the factory, ensuring that Daffin's continues to live up to its fine reputation.

When you've had your fill of the Chocolate Kingdom, spend an hour or so wandering through the company's attractive retail space, a kind of candy memory lane. Every variety of sweet is for sale, including

Making Cherry Cordials

Consider the challenge of cherry cordials. The solid center is no problem, but how do you coat that liquidy layer with chocolate?

Some manufacturers form the chocolate shell upside down, squirt the centers and the liquid in, then coat the bottom, which at this point is on top, with chocolate. They let the whole thing cool, then unmold the finished candy.

Others, like Daffin's Candies, take advantage of a series of chemical reactions. A blend of sugar, corn syrup, and water is cooked at about 250 degrees. When the mixture becomes thin and sticky, kind of like syrup, it goes into a cooling drum. Some of the cooked mixture is removed and saved for later use. The rest finishes cooling and is moved to a mixer.

As the powerful mixer does its work, crystals in the sugar are stretched. The syrup thickens into a white paste. Flavoring and invertase, an enzyme, are added, and the mixture is now known as fondant. The hot syrup that was decanted earlier is now added back in, which helps soften the fondant. Half-ounce maraschino cherries are placed in a revolving pan, where they are completely coated with fondant. The whole thing cools, and the fondant crystallizes until it is very hard, not mushy or liquid at all. The cherry-fondant combination can then be enrobed in chocolate.

So how does the liquid form? It's thanks to the invertase, with a little help from the cherry. This enzyme makes the candy cordialize, or become liquid. Invertase works on sucrose, breaking down its crystal structure. The cherry holds a little bit of syrup when it's placed in the candy, and the invertase uses this to help soften the fondant; without the cherry, the fondant would soften but not liquefy. It takes about two weeks for the invertase to convert the fondant completely. The result is the sweet, creamy liquid that Daffin's cordials are renowned for.

Chocolate comes to life at Daffin's Chocolate Kingdom. PHOTO BY KYLE R. WEAVER

cases of chocolates fresh from Daffin's factory. The shop also has a large Hallmark department, so there is a wide selection of cards and related items, and Daffin's supplies more than fifty Hallmark and other gift stores with fine chocolates. If your friends and family have special occasions coming up, this is the perfect one-stop shopping venue for finding gifts and cards for everybody. You can even have packages sent directly to the recipients.

For anyone overwhelmed by the plethora of choices, Daffin's recommends the Jean Marie Chocolate Collection, a favorite hand-molded assortment. Made with chocolates ranging from delicate milk chocolate to a deep, dark chocolate, the candies contain scrumptious centers like whole nuts, truffles, and opera creams.

Curious about how these confections are created? Take the factory tour and get a close-up view of old-fashioned candy making the Daffin's way.

The Tour

The tour begins with a short videotape, "Affection for Confection," which you watch standing. Along with a brief history of chocolate in

Visiting Daffin's Candies

SHARON, PA

Fax number: 724-342-7623

E-mail address: order@daffins.com

Tour hours: Monday–Friday, 9 A.M.– 3 P.M. September–May; tours run Tuesday–Thursday, 9 A.M.–3 P.M. June–August; some weeks in summer, no tours are scheduled. Chocolate Kingdom is open Monday–Saturday, 9 A.M.–9 P.M.; Sunday, 11 A.M.–5 P.M.

Admission: Free.

Reservations: Required at least two weeks in advance for factory tour.

Special considerations: Wheelchair accessible. No age restrictions. Strollers permitted. Still and video cameras permitted. The tour goes through a working factory. Wear closed-toed, nonskid shoes.

Tour length and type: 35-minute guided tour on the factory floor. Plan to spend at least a half hour in the retail store and Chocolate Kingdom.

Group size: Maximum of thirty people. Larger groups will be split, and groups of fifteen or fewer people may be combined. Individuals and families welcome.

On-site facilities: Candy store, restrooms.

Special events: The best time to visit is during the month before Easter. Swizzle Stick Day is held the Sunday before Palm Sunday.

Nearby attractions: Contact the Mercer County Convention and Visitors Bureau at 800-637-2370 or visit the website www.mercercountypa.org for information about Mercer County attractions. These include the Avenue of 444 Flags, the Canal Museum, Pymatuning Deer Park, Reyer's (the "world's largest" shoe store), Wendell August Gift Shoppe and Forge, and the Winner (the "world's largest" off-price women's clothing store). Visitors are welcome at Philadelphia Candies in nearby Hermitage.

Directions: To reach the factory, from I-80, take Exit 1 North to Farrell. Continue to Daffin's Chocolate Factory on Spearman Avenue. The factory is on the right. To reach the main retail store, from I-80, take Exit 1 North to Farrell, past the factory store. This road is Broadway. Turn right onto State Street after passing the PA Route 62 bypass. Daffin's Candies/Chocolate Kingdom is on the right.

general and Daffin's operation in particular, the tape quotes Swedish botanist Carolus Linnaeus, who termed chocolate "the food of gods."

Then you are invited into the production area. Two 10,000-pound chocolate tanks hold the raw material—which arrives at the factories in 1,500-pound cartons—so that it can be piped throughout the system. At any given time, 30,000 pounds of chocolate can be in the works, with every type of candy requiring a different recipe. Creamy centers and smooth caramels cook slowly in huge copper kettles to mouth-watering consistency.

It's fascinating to learn the ins and outs of confectionery manufacture. You'll get a chance to see an automated cluster dipper, molds that are filled and then removed after a trip through the cooling tunnel, and the chocolate coating line. To coat the candy on the bottom, a conveyor belt takes the centers up a melted chocolate hill. Then they travel under a chocolate shower that drenches the rest of them completely.

Here's another well-kept secret. You can tell what kind of center is inside a coated candy without sticking your fingernail in the bottom or taking a bite. Each piece has a code on top. "Hand strung" chocolates are decorated on top by a real person. The pattern of melted chocolate on the candy—three squiggles, an X, a spiral, whatever—identifies what's inside. Each candy company uses a different code, however.

A favorite part of the tour, especially at busy times, is the stop at the bar line, where up to three thousand chocolate bars are wrapped per hour. In the packing area, candy is weighed, packed, and shrink-wrapped in boxes ranging from 6 ounces to 5 pounds. Packers can finish up to 300 pounds per hour.

There are some gigantic chocolate animals here, too. You'll want to take pictures of the seven-foot-tall rabbit and the chubby apatosaurus, among others.

Everyone gets a sample at the end of the tour, and there's a store at the factory site where you can purchase more. The Sunday before Palm Sunday is the annual Swizzle Stick Day, a factory open house with free swizzle sticks dipped in fresh chocolate dispensed from the milk chocolate fountain all day. Clowns, dressed characters, balloons, and music entertain visitors. Everyone gets a factory tour and the chance to watch Easter confections being decorated with exquisite hand piping. The event, like Daffin's, is a real treat.

Sherm Edwards Candies

509 Cavitt Avenue
Trafford, PA 15085-1060
412-372-4331 or
    800-436-5424

Sherm Edwards Candies and the borough of Trafford where the company is located have a lot in common. They've both been around for a while. Both have seen their share of economic ups and downs and have found creative ways to survive and thrive in changing conditions. And most importantly, their foundation of quality bodes well for their future.

The company's founder, Sherm Edwards, got started in the candy business in 1946, working for the Keystone Candy Company in Lawrenceville, which was owned by his then father-in-law, Charlie Sarandou. Edwards spent twenty-one years there, then started his own custom candy concern on East Ohio Street on Pittsburgh's North Side.

Edwards realized early on that he couldn't compete pricewise with the major manufacturers, so he instead chose to emphasize quality. "Good candy is not cheap and cheap candy is not good" is the company motto.

When Sherm Edwards Candies got too big for its North Side location, the company found other Pittsburgh properties prohibitively expensive. A search in the suburbs led Sherm Edwards to Trafford in 1977, a town that straddles Allegheny and Westmoreland Counties. Trafford began with George Westinghouse's purchase of 17 acres here in 1902. His plan was to build a company town, named Trafford City after the site of one of his English factories.

Cavitt Avenue, where Sherm Edwards Candies now stands, was part of a planned commercial district carved from that land. In its heyday, Cavitt Avenue was alive with businesses: taverns and pool rooms, a bowling alley and a movie theater, a photography studio and a printer's shop, a drugstore and medical offices.

But as Westinghouse Electric Corporation began to falter in the 1970s, Trafford suffered too. The circuit breaker division closed for good in the early 1980s, with a devastating impact on the town. The population declined, with a concomitant effect on property tax revenues.

Fortunately, that's not the end of the story. Trafford's population decline slowed, then reversed, as young families started noticing the town's reasonable tax structures, affordable housing, and good school district. Town leaders and volunteers worked to improve Trafford's recreational facilities and business climate.

Sherm Edwards Candies played a key part in the renaissance of Cavitt Avenue. Edwards purchased the defunct McBride Theater, sold the projectors and seats, and refurbished the building, putting the candy factory in the basement and a retail candy shop and offices on the first floor. Sherm Edwards Candies opened its Trafford store on December 8, 1978.

Like the town, Edwards was always ready to try something new for an economic shot in the arm. He considered adding retail space to the business, maybe in a mall, but financial analyses showed that that wouldn't be cost-effective. Instead, Edwards increased his wholesale and fund-raising business.

Most chocolates at Sherm Edwards Candies go through the enrobing line twice.

He also began some serious promotion for the factory tour. Busloads—sometimes more than three hundred in a year—would visit Sherm Edwards Candies, touring the facility and spending money in the retail store. The bus trade has slowed somewhat since two local hotels have stopped arranging bus tours for groups staying at their facilities, but a stop at Sherm Edwards Candies is still on the list for many tours that visit the area. Individuals and families are also discovering how much fun it is to see a real custom candy shop in operation.

Edwards gave a lot to the candy business, and he got a lot back. At a Cincinnati trade show in 1975, the candy maker met Dorothy Golembeski, the owner of Golem Candies in

Visiting Sherm Edwards Candies

TRAFFORD, PA

Fax number: 412-373-8089

E-mail address:
dgolembeski@earthlink.net

Tour hours: Monday–Friday, 9 A.M.–
3 P.M. (Closed Mondays, and sometimes other days, in summer). Store
open Monday–Saturday, 9 A.M.–4 P.M.

Admission: Free.

Reservations: Required.

Special considerations: Retail store
is wheelchair accessible, but the tour
requires guests to walk down a flight
of steps. There is no elevator. No age
restrictions. Strollers permitted in the
retail store, but not on the tour. Still
and video cameras permitted. The
tour goes through a working factory.
Wear closed-toed, nonskid shoes.

Tour length and type: 45 minutes
to 1 hour and 15 minutes. Guided
factory tour.

Group size: Maximum of forty to fifty
people per tour (full bus). Individuals
and families welcome, but small
groups may be combined.

On-site facilities: Retail store.

Special events: The best time to visit
is between Labor Day and Easter.
All You Can Eat party in autumn, $5
for an hour and a half in the factory
and retail store.

Nearby attractions: Contact the Greater
Pittsburgh Convention and Visitors
Bureau at 800-366-0093 or visit the
website www.visitpittsburgh.com for
information about Allegheny County
attractions, including Kennywood
Park, Westinghouse Museum in
Wilmerding, and Pittsburgh cultural
attractions.

Directions: From the Pittsburgh Exit
(6/37) of the Pennsylvania Turnpike,
take PA Business Route 22 West
about 100 yards to PA Route 48
South. Stay on Route 48 for about 3.5
miles to PA Route 130 South. Take
Route 130 about 1 mile to Trafford. Go
over the bridge into town, then turn left
onto Brinton Avenue. Turn right at the
next corner onto Sixth Street, then
turn right again onto the one-way
Cavitt Avenue. Sherm Edwards is
on the right-hand side about halfway
down the block.

nearby Pitcairn. The two combined not only their candy stores, but also their lives when they married a year later.

Sherm Edwards died in August 1999, but his company and his town continue to flourish. There's a sense of optimism that it will continue to be so. Dorothy is still involved in the business, and her son David Golembeski now owns Sherm Edwards Candies.

The Tour

After a brief introduction from your tour guide, you are invited to descend the stairs to the 40-by-90-foot factory. One whiff tells you that this is old-fashioned candy making at its best. It might be the aroma of roasting coconut, the scent of sweet strawberries, or the rich bouquet of melted chocolate.

Sherm Edwards Candies blends its own milk chocolate and two types of dark chocolate from raw materials supplied by chocolate manufacturers Blommer, Guittard, and Wilbur. (White chocolate comes from Wilbur, too.) The chocolate is melted and mixed in 500-pound melters. When it's the right consistency, workers carry it in buckets to where it's needed, either in the molding area or to one of three enrobing lines. Like most manufacturers, Sherm Edwards Candies carries a large variety of molds from which customers can choose.

Gleaming copper kettles are the heart of the kitchen area, where candy centers, caramels, and fudge are made. The 80-quart mixers, like everything else in the busy factory, are spick-and-span.

Watching the enrobing process is a highlight of the tour. The day I visited, workers were making stolen heaven: a conglomeration of marshmallow, pecans, and chocolate. After its first coating on the conveyor belt, each piece was meticulously hand inspected to look for uncoated spots on the bottom, which could cause a center to leak or to dry out. Almost all Sherm Edwards chocolates receive a double coating, just to be on the safe side.

Although chocolate is not manufactured here from cacao beans (most small candy makers purchase chocolate from large companies), the guide does explain the chocolate-making process. Large photos of cacao pods and beans, the drying process, roasting, and shelling provide a good general introduction. Interestingly, cocoa powder has a distinctive taste based on the origin of the beans and the way they've been roasted.

The guide offers samples during and after the tour. When you bite into a sample fresh off the line, think about the tradition of care and quality that went into it.

Gardners Candies

30 West Tenth Street
Tyrone, PA 16686
814-684-0857
www.gardnerscandies.com

Back in 1910 candy-making entrepreneur James A. "Pike" Gardner created the first heart-shaped box for Valentine candy. Gardner's boxes weren't the run-of-the mill red cardboard throwaways we're used to today. They were beautiful, ornate works of art, padded and quilted with satin, decorated imaginatively with ribbons, buttons, and bows, collector's items to anyone who was lucky enough to receive one. Some look like tuxedo shirts complete with ruffles. Others are standard heart shapes, but nothing about the embellishments on them could be called standard. These boxes are special.

Even if you don't have a box like this among your family heirlooms, you can still view and admire them. They're on display at Gardners Candies in Tyrone, showcased as part of a one-room candy-making museum done up as an old-time candy kitchen, in a building that also holds Gardners retail shop, penny candy store, and an ice-cream parlor. Sarris Candies of Canonsburg purchased Gardners in 1997. Gardners still makes its own delicious candy under its own name.

The nearby factory doesn't give tours, but the Tenth Street site shows a video of the production process for anyone who wants to see what Pike put into those gorgeous boxes.

The Tour

The fifteen-minute video presentation is hosted by a guide who takes some young friends back in time to an old-fashioned candy store. After some background on Pike Gardner's 1897 start in business, the guide explains the company's evolution. From its original 800 square feet of floor space, the firm has grown tremendously. Currently, the factory alone has more than 50,000 square feet.

In 1959, the company got out of the wholesale market to concentrate on making its own candies. A second store was opened in nearby State College in 1962, the same year that Gardners bought a chocolate-

Some of the many beautiful Valentine's Day candy boxes on display at Gardners Candies.

coating machine. In 1976, Gardners added a factory in Bald Eagle, where its signature peanut butter meltaway was perfected. Eight years later, the company invested in a machine that could make 15,000 pounds of meltaways every day. The cost: $1 million.

The film of the factory shows chocolate being delivered in boxes that contain 150 10-pound blocks. Into the melter it goes, 2,500 pounds at a time. The melted chocolate is then pumped to the coating room.

Meanwhile, candy cream centers are being made by hand in the kitchen. Just like in the old days, sweet concoctions in copper kettles are heated over gas fires to 246 degrees. When the centers are ready, they're poured into a beater to cool and solidify. As the temperature drops to 110 degrees, beating begins. This is also when the flavors are added. The mixture begins to cream up and is separated into smaller loaves, then sent through a press that makes forty-eight centers at a time. The finished centers wait on candy boards until the outsides crystallize.

Melted chocolate and centers come together in the enrobing process. The centers are placed on a conveyor moving at 8 feet per minute. This carries the candies over a puddle of chocolate to coat them on the bottom. A cold plate hardens the chocolate, then the bottoms are coated again before the top-coating procedure starts. An enrobing line produces about 120 pounds of candies per hour. Finished pieces are hand strung, marked by hand with a distinctive pattern of melted chocolate on top to identify what kind of center is inside.

After the candies cool in a 40-foot tunnel, they're packed. Each kind of candy is put in a separate section of a Ferris wheel–like packing machine. Workers wait until the packing wheel brings them the right kind of candy for their boxes. Full boxes are weighed, dated, and wrapped in cellophane.

Of the more than three hundred types of candy Gardners makes, far and away the most popular is the peanut butter meltaway. In the melt-away-making machine, spouts inside of spouts take turns—fractions of a second apart—squirting chocolate, then soft, creamy peanut butter, then chocolate again into waiting receptacles. Just like toy soldiers, the candies march in straight lines through the production area.

After the video, linger for a while in the candy museum, where time seems to have been turned back a hundred years. It's nicely laid out so that you can get close to everything and even touch some of it. Look for the store's original "air-conditioning"—a ceiling fan. There are also an old ice chest, candy thermometers, taffy hooks, and antique tin boxes.

One display case holds candy molds made of German silver. This

Visiting Gardners
TYRONE, PA

Fax number: 814-684-2034

E-mail address: Directly through website, www.gardnerscandies.com

Tour hours: Monday–Saturday, 9:30 A.M.–9 P.M.; Sunday, 1 P.M.–9 P.M. year-round. Closed major holidays.

Admission: Free.

Reservations: Groups of twenty or more must call to reserve at least twenty-four hours in advance.

Special considerations: Wheelchair accessible front and back entrances and restrooms. No age restrictions. Strollers permitted. Still and video cameras permitted.

Tour length and type: 15-minute video of production, and about 15 more minutes to take the self-guided tour through candy museum.

Group size: Maximum of fifty people per tour. Individuals and families welcome.

On-site facilities: Candy shop, ice cream parlor, restrooms.

Nearby attractions: Contact the Allegheny Mountains Convention and Visitors Bureau at 800-84-ALTOONA or visit the website www.allegheny mountains.com for information about Tyrone-area attractions, including Altoona Railroaders Memorial Museum, Bland's Park, Horseshoe Curve National Historic Landmark, Indian Caverns, Lincoln Caverns, Pennsylvania State University, and Raystown Lake.

Directions: Exit I-99 at Tyrone. Follow the off-ramp to the right, which leads toward town. Gardners Candies is on the right after the traffic light.

Gardners Candies's penny candy store-within-a-store.

material was used because it gave the finished molded chocolate a lovely sheen. Today, Gardners Easter bunnies are still made in German molds. The company has about a thousand molds in various sizes and shapes.

A large glass shadow box in the center of the room holds postcards, advertisements, letters, and newspaper articles, along with a pictorial explanation of how cacao beans are made into chocolate and other relevant items. Behind the candy museum is Gardners ice cream parlor, a perfect place to cool off on a hot day. On the other side of the museum room, toward the front entrance, is a penny candy counter. It's a re-created circa 1900 candy shop stocked with classic candies such as fireballs and licorice whips.

The large, more contemporary retail space up front sells Gardners products, including candies molded in shapes ranging from computers to pickles. Purchase a bag of goodies and start thinking about how nice it would be to pack some in a beautiful box for your loved one next Valentine's Day.

Hershey's Chocolate World

800 Park Boulevard
Hershey, PA 17033-0800
717-534-4900
www.HersheysChocolateWorld.com

Like thousands of other people who toured the Hershey's chocolate manufacturing plant during the forty-four years that it was open for tours, I felt betrayed when the factory doors at 19 East Chocolate Avenue closed to visitors in 1973. But recently, I decided to put my bad attitude on hold and give Chocolate World a chance. I smelled the chocolate aroma being piped through the building. I took the chocolate-making tour ride, starring me as a cacao bean. I got my free sample of chocolate. I explored the tropical garden area, marveled at how much Hershey's merchandise there was in the shops, smiled at the costumed characters as they strutted past, and got a surprisingly tasty dinner in the food court. And you know what? It was fun.

Sure, it's different than it was in the old days, when you could see huge vats of liquid chocolate being stirred right before your eyes, but that's okay. For a virtual factory tour, there's none better than Hershey's. Perhaps that's why Chocolate World is the most highly attended corporate visitors center in the country, with more than 50 million visitors passing through since it opened almost thirty years ago.

A visit to Chocolate World is a fun and educational way to learn about the way Hershey's products are made and how the company grew from a one-man operation to a huge, multinational corporation. There is so much to see and do in Hershey; try to make this a more than one-day vacation destination if you can.

Milton Snavely Hershey (1857–1945) lived the American dream. He was born to Mennonite parents in Derry Township. Mother and father did not get along, and the family moved several times before landing in Lancaster County. From age fourteen to eighteen, Hershey apprenticed with a Lancaster confectioner, where he showed a talent for candy making.

By the time he was eighteen, Hershey opened his own candy business in Philadelphia. It failed, leading him to move to Denver to try sil-

How Chocolate Is Made

Today, cacao trees are grown chiefly in western Africa, with Ghana, Côte d'Ivoire, Nigeria, and Cameroon the leading producers, as well as Brazil and Ecuador.

Cacao trees need protection from wind and sun, especially for the first few years of growth. Cultivated trees usually begin to bear fruit in their fifth year. After that, a tree can yield several harvests a year.

The average tree reaches about 20 feet, has shiny leaves up to 12 inches long, and produces small, pink flowers. The purple or off-white seeds are enclosed in a yellow or reddish brown pod. Individually, they resemble almonds, but when they're embedded in the pulpy mass inside their pods they look like teeth from a *Tyrannosaurus rex*. Inside the seeds are oily, bitter, brown kernels. Those are the cocoa beans. It takes about four hundred cocoa beans to make 1 pound of chocolate.

The process of turning cocoa beans into chocolate is so complex that it's amazing anyone ever figured it out. Beans are fermented, during which time the enzymes bring out their chocolate flavor. Then they're dried in the sun, cleaned, and roasted. The roasting separates the bean's shell from the center, or nib.

Nibs are ground into chocolate liquor. This free-flowing liquid contains no alcohol, but it does contain about 50 percent cocoa butter, the basic component in chocolate. The cocoa butter is extracted

ver mining. This effort, too, was a flop. He then got a job with a Denver candy maker. Here he learned to make caramels with fresh milk, a skill he later put to good use. Hershey opened another candy business in New York City in 1883 but was unsuccessful once again. The broke twenty-nine-year-old returned to Lancaster.

Hershey's next venture was the Lancaster Caramel Company, supported largely by his mother, aunt, and one former employee. A lucky break came when a British candy importer agreed to sell the caramels abroad. Hershey was able to secure bank funding so that he could buy from the chocolate liquor by giant presses. This leaves a solid mass of pure cocoa, called press cake. The cake is ground and refined.

For milk chocolate, milk and sugar are condensed to the consistency of taffy. Chocolate liquor is added, and the combination is mixed until it forms a dry, coarse powder called chocolate crumb. Additional cocoa butter is added to make the chocolate creamy and rich.

After passing through steel rollers that reduce the particle size of the blended ingredients, the chocolate goes through the conching process, so named because the vats used to be shaped like shells. Conching mixes and refines the chocolate by using giant rollers that move back and forth through the chocolate for up to seventy-two hours. The resulting product can be molded into bars, either for consumption or for use in making other candy.

Because it is so complicated, not to mention expensive and time-consuming, to make chocolate, it's no surprise that this is done only at a few very large companies. Only two of the companies in this book actually make their own chocolate: Hershey Foods Corporation and Wilbur Chocolate Company. The other candy makers get chocolate from them or from other large manufacturers such as Nestlé, Blommer, or Guittard. It may come in the form of huge cartons of 10-pound chocolate bars that will be melted down or liquid chocolate that's been trucked in to waiting roof tanks. Many candy makers purchase chocolate from several sources, then create their own blend to achieve a unique taste.

equipment and ingredients. Within four years, Hershey had made his first million. A candy empire was born.

In 1898, the forty-one-year-old Hershey married Catherine "Kitty" Sweeney. The Hersheys shared their wealth through numerous philanthropic efforts, donating funds to Franklin and Marshall College in Lancaster, St. Patrick's Cathedral in Harrisburg, and the model community that would eventually be known as Hershey, Pennsylvania.

In 1903, plans were made for a new town, which would have a population of fifteen hundred. Centered around a new chocolate factory, the town was designed to combine business and pleasure so that people could work successfully and live well. Hershey encouraged home ownership, built an infrastructure, supported civic institutions, and had his company manage utilities and recreational facilities. His model town soon got the nickname of Chocolatetown, U.S.A.

Hershey consolidated one-room schoolhouses into a new school, created zoning that would exclude public or commercial buildings from residential areas, and had the entire town landscaped. Kitty Hershey encouraged her husband to open a school for orphaned boys, and in 1909, the Hershey Industrial School—now coeducational and called the Milton Hershey School—opened. The institution's goal was to provide a homelike atmosphere and an education. By the early 1930s, the school had twenty-two dormitories, each housing up to twenty-eight boys.

The Hershey American Indian Museum, now the Hershey Museum, was completed in 1933. The Hotel Hershey was opened that same year on a hill overlooking the town. Three years later, the Hershey Sports Arena opened to house the Hershey Bears team of the Eastern Amateur Hockey League.

In 1937, Hershey decided to create a garden for local residents to enjoy. He opened a 3½-acre rose garden to the public; this would eventually be expanded to a 23-acre display with an award-winning rose garden as its centerpiece.

Throughout the years, the chocolate company continued to thrive, even through wartime and the Depression. When Hershey died on October 13, 1945 (predeceased by his wife in 1915), he left a robust company, one of the giants in the food industry. Subsequent management expanded the company and its product line and, in 1968, reorganized the corporation into Hershey Foods Corporation. In 1981, Hershey Chocolate Company, the corporation's largest division, posted $1 billion in annual sales.

Today, Hershey Foods Corporation has international operations in more than ninety countries. It holds the top position nationally in chocolate and nonchocolate confections.

Throughout the town, with its charming Hershey's Kisses lampposts and well-manicured parks, you can see the results of how Milton Hershey used his financial success as a springboard to accomplish the goals that

Costumed characters greet visitors to Hershey's Chocolate World. COURTESY OF
HERSHEY'S CHOCOLATE WORLD

were near to his heart. Hershey Entertainment and Resort Company
(HERCO) owns and operates HersheyPark, HersheyPark Arena, ZooAmer-
ica North American Wildlife Park, Hershey Bears American Hockey
League Club, Hershey Wildcats professional soccer team, the Hotel Hershey, Hershey Lodge and Convention Center, and Hershey Highmeadow
Campground. The Milton Hershey School continues to house and edu-
cate more than eleven hundred financially and socially needy students.
The M. S. Hershey Foundation, begun in 1935, supports education and
cultural enrichment for the local area. The Milton S. Hershey Medical
Center of the Pennsylvania State University was founded on funds from
the Hershey foundation. Milton S. Hershey's legacy is visible at every turn
in the pretty, chocolate-scented town that bears his name.

Hershey's Kisses are probably the company's best-known confections. The first kisses were made in 1907, named perhaps for the sound
the chocolate made as it was squirted onto a conveyor belt. Early kisses
were wrapped by hand, but machine wrapping supplanted hand wrapping in 1921. Always looking to get the Hershey's name in the forefront,

Visiting Hershey's Chocolate World

HERSHEY, PA

Fax number: 717-534-5730

Tour hours: Vary depending on season. Open year-round, except Christmas Day. Check brochure or website www.HersheysChocolateWorld.com

Admission: Free.

Reservations: Recommended for groups of twenty or more.

Special considerations: Accessible for standard wheelchairs. Wheelchairs can be borrowed at the front desk. Users of electric wheelchairs can watch an alternate video. Restaurant and restrooms are accessible. No age restrictions. Strollers are not permitted on tour ride, but there's a covered stroller-check area outside. Still and video photography permitted.

Tour length and type: 15-minute amusement park–type ride.

Group size: No maximum number of people, but large groups will have to split up in the ride cars. Seven people can fit in one car. Individuals and families welcome.

On-site facilities: Restrooms, food court, full-service restaurant, numerous shops selling Hershey's products and other related merchandise.

Special events: Include Creatures of the Night, Balloonfest, Halloween in Hershey, Christmas Candylane, and others. Call for specifics.

Nearby attractions: Contact the Harrisburg–Hershey–Carlisle–Perry County Tourism and Convention Bureau at 800-995-0969 or visit the website www.visithhc.com for information on attractions, including Cornwall Iron Furnace, Hershey Gardens, Hershey Museum, HersheyPark, Indian Echo Caverns, the State Capitol, and the State Museum of Pennsylvania. In nearby Palmyra, Seltzer's Smokehouse Meats also welcomes guests for a short video tour.

Directions: From the Lebanon-Lancaster Exit (20/266) of the Pennsylvania Turnpike, take U.S. Route 322 West. After you cross U.S. Route 422 (Chocolate Avenue), the road is called HersheyPark Drive. Look for signs directing you to Chocolate World parking, or to HersheyPark parking if you will be going there, too.

From I-83 or the Harrisburg East (19/247) Exit of the Pennsylvania Turnpike, take U.S. Route 322 East. Turn left onto HersheyPark Drive. Look for signs directing you to Chocolate World parking, or to HersheyPark parking if you will be going there, too.

Hershey added the paper Hershey's tag to the product and even obtained a trademark for this type of plume sticking out of a candy wrapper. Today, the factory cranks out more than 70 million kiss-shaped products every day.

Over the years, many products were introduced. Some disappeared almost as soon as they had emerged; others, like Hershey's Kisses, have enjoyed decades of popularity. The former category includes the Mild and Mellow bar, the Aero chocolate bar, the butter chip bar, and chocolate-covered candy-coated peanuts. The latter group encompasses favorites like Mr. Goodbar, introduced in 1925; Krackel, which debuted in 1938; and Hershey's instant cocoa. In 1963, Hershey Chocolate acquired the H. B. Reese Candy Co., Inc.; products in this line eventually included peanut butter cups, Reese's Pieces, peanut butter (smooth and crunchy), and Nutrageous. Six years later, Hershey Foods Corporation signed a marketing and manufacturing agreement with Rowntree MacKintosh, which enabled Hershey to make and sell Kit Kat and Rolo in the United States.

In 1983, Hershey's chocolate milk was introduced, the first premixed chocolate drink sold by the company. In 1988, Hershey Foods Corporation acquired Cadbury Schweppes's U.S. confectionery operations, with products including York Peppermint Patties, Peter Paul Mounds and Almond Joy, and Cadbury brand-name items.

Its pattern of innovation and expansion for almost a century has given Hershey Foods a reputation as the maker of "the great American chocolate bar"—and so much more.

The Tour

Chocolate World's tour ride was renovated in 1998, with comfortable cars and clear-as-a-bell audio. Once you're seated, the ride takes you to the equator, where cocoa beans are harvested. When the beans arrive at the Hershey factory, they're sorted by country. You feel the heat that simulates the 400-degree roaster that the real beans go through to develop their flavor and aroma.

A key ingredient in Hershey's products is milk. Central Pennsylvania has many dairy farms, so the company has a plentiful local supply. The ride takes you past a mooing cow, an animated counterpart to the real-life bovines that provide Hershey's with more than 235,000 gallons of milk every day.

As the ride proceeds, you become acquainted with terms like nibs, the inner meat of the cocoa bean; chocolate liquor, a free-flowing, alcohol-free liquid created after the nibs are milled; and chocolate crumb, the coarse powder that results when sweetened, condensed milk is mixed with chocolate liquor, then dried.

It's impressive to watch massive steel rollers pulverize the ingredients into a smooth chocolate paste. The paste is then mixed and refined in the conching process. Giant granite rollers move back and forth, mixing chocolate in boxlike containers. This goes on for up to seventy-two hours, making the chocolate silky smooth.

You watch Hershey's chocolate being molded into bars and a machine squirting out tray after tray of Hershey Kisses, to the tune of 70 million kiss-shaped products every day.

As the ride ends, posters of old-time and contemporary advertisements join pictures of happy people eating Hershey's products. You'll likely be surprised at just how many brands of candy are actually made by Hershey Foods Corporation. As music plays, exit to receive your candy sample and visit the rest of Chocolate World.

Philadelphia Candies

1546 East State Street
Hermitage, PA 16148
724-981-6341
www.philadelphiacandies.com

The first thing everyone wants to know about Philadelphia Candies is why it's called Philadelphia when it's at the opposite end of the state from that large city. The answer has to do with the meaning of the word, not the metropolis. Derived from the Greek, the word means "brotherly love." Philadelphia Candies was founded in 1919 by two Greek immigrants, brothers Jim and Steve Macris, and the name of their company represents their close relationship.

Philadelphia Candies is located in a small shopping center that's easy to miss. It's worth making the effort to find it, however, as it's a candy-making gem. The 4,000-square-foot retail space up front attractively displays more than 300 types of fresh chocolate creations that are made in the 30,000-square-foot factory just beyond the back door. The store is an attractive combination of old-fashioned and modern, in a way that makes it feel very welcoming. Simple, elegant ceiling fixtures supplement fluorescent lighting, and the contemporary checkered inlay on the floor contrasts nicely with the octagonal-shaped tiles that were popular in the mid-twentieth century. Neatly stacked rows of candies are shown off in gleaming glass cases and jars similar to the ones that proprietors favored in the days of the general store. Classical music adds just the right touch.

Two other Macris brothers, Louis and John, later joined Jim and Steve in the business. Today, Spyros Macris, John's son, operates the business with his wife, Georgia, continuing the Shenango Valley tradition that's been maintained for more than eighty years.

The Tour

Most candy stores smell good, but one with a factory in the back smells incredible. Your tour starts in the Philadelphia Candies warehouse. A tank holds up to 7,000 pounds of melted chocolate, which travels to its destination through stainless steel piping.

The kitchen isn't always on the tour, but it will be if you're lucky. (Ask about this when your tour starts, and your request will probably be granted.) Here you'll see gleaming copper kettles that are used to make creams and caramels, fudges, and marshmallow and egg fillings.

Next, it's on to the molding area. It's fun to watch liquid chocolate squirt into a mold, then see the bubbles shimmied out by a vibrating machine. The sealed mold passes through a cooler to set the chocolate before

the mold is opened. The size of the mold determines how long it takes for the chocolate to cool. Philadelphia Candies has a mold for just about anything, from teddy bears and turtles to cars and trucks. They make custom novelties and are happy to consider special requests.

It's easy to tell what season it is by looking at what's coming off the production line. Before Christmas, solid hand-decorated chocolate reindeer, Santas, and trees are plentiful. Easter features chocolate rabbits, from bite-size to taller than 3 feet, and hand-decorated chocolate baskets almost too pretty to eat. The closer you look, the more detail you notice, and the

Philadelphia Candies' molded and filled chocolates are a local tradition. COURTESY OF PHILADELPHIA CANDIES

Visiting
Philadelphia Candies

HERMITAGE, PA

Fax number: 724-981-6490

Tour hours: Monday–Friday,
9 A.M.–4 P.M. year-round. Store
open Monday–Saturday, 9 A.M.–9 P.M.;
Sunday, 11 A.M.–5 P.M.

Admission: Free.

Reservations: Required, except
for the annual open-house tour.

Special considerations: Wheelchair
accessible. No age restrictions.
Strollers permitted. Photography is
discouraged. The tour goes through
a working factory. Wear closed-toed,
nonskid shoes.

Tour length and type: 15-minute
guided tour of the factory floor.

Group size: Maximum of forty people.
Individuals and families welcome.
Small groups may be combined.

On-site facilities: Retail store.

Special events: The best time to visit
is mid-September through the end of
March. Open-house tour two Sundays
before Easter.

Nearby attractions: Contact the Mercer
County Convention and Visitors Bureau
at 800-637-2370 or visit the website
www.mercercountypa.org for information about Mercer County attractions.
These include the Avenue of 444 Flags,
the Canal Museum, Pymatuning Deer
Park, Reyer's (the "world's largest"
shoe store), Wendell August Gift
Shoppe and Forge, and the Winner
(the "world's largest" off-price women's
clothing store). Visitors are also welcome at Daffin's Candies retail shop
and Chocolate Kingdom in Sharon,
and at Daffin's factory in Farrell.

Directions: From the intersection of I-79
and I-80, take I-80 west to the Sharon
Exit, PA Route 18. Take Route 18
North, crossing U.S. Route 62. Turn
left onto Business Route 62. Philadelphia Candies is in a shopping center
on the left between Buhl Farm Drive
and Smith Avenue.

more you appreciate the artistry and
steady hands it takes to fashion something like this. *McCall's* magazine featured the chocolate baskets in a March
1991 article, "Easter Basket Treats."

In the enrober room, you see candies pushed through a chocolate "puddle" to get coated underneath. They
travel over a cooling plate to set up the
chocolate on the bottom, then are
drenched in chocolate that pours from
above. One of Philadelphia Candies'
most popular items, especially among
the locals, is the croquette, a confection
with a butter cream center, covered in
chocolate, then rolled in nuts. Philadelphia Candies hand designs the dark
chocolates, with a person using a finger
to drip a special insignia on each piece.
Each type of candy has a unique signature; if you learn them, you can tell
what's inside before you take a bite.

Two Saturdays before Easter,
Philadelphia Candies opens the tour to
one and all. The Easter bunny makes
an appearance, along with other costumed characters to entertain folks as
they wait in line. As on the scheduled
tours, everyone gets a sample. Built on
brotherly love and a tradition of quality, the Macrises enjoy sharing the
sweeter things in life with their guests.

Pulakos 926 Chocolates

2530 Parade Street
Erie, PA 16503
814-452-4026 or 800-627-0926
www.pulakoschocolates.com

George P. Pulakos opened his Erie candy factory in 1903, the same year that the Wright Flyer made its first successful flight. Since then, the aviation industry has thrived; so has Pulakos 926 Chocolates, where four generations of the family have combined the art and science of candy making to create a superior product well known in the region.

After George P., son Constantine "Gus" took over the business, followed by Gus's son, Achilles "Herk," who ran the firm for decades. The current president, George A. Pulakos, took over after Herk died in February 2000.

The original store was located at 1108 State Street in Erie. Five years later, Pulakos Chocolates moved to 926 State Street. Along with the candy operation, 926 boasted a restaurant, bakery, and soda fountain. The manufacturing facility on Parade Street is exclusively candy; the quintessential Art Deco lettering style on the sign over the door is a beautiful reminder of the company's long history. Two of the other three Pulakos sites sell candy only, but the West 26th Street and Elmwood Avenue location also offers Pulakos's original ice cream from May through October.

Pulakos is so respected in the industry that it serves as the site for the Retail Confectioners International/Gus Pulakos Short Course in Retail Candymaking, a comprehensive, two-week course offered every other year to experienced candy makers, in conjunction with Gannon University. In this intensive program, with its demanding curriculum, classes run from 7:30 A.M. until 5 P.M., with hands-on training in subjects like creams, fondants, frappes, sanitation, and humectants (dealing with moisture in candy).

"We have a faculty of industry experts numbering around thirty," says George Pulakos. "There's a chocolate team, a sugar man, flavors people, machinery people, a technician from a fats and oils company, and so on." Enrollment is limited to twenty-four students, which ensures that everyone has a chance to speak with the instructors and consultants. Applications start arriving a year in advance from all over the world, and they've had students from as far away as Australia and Saudi Arabia.

It was Herk Pulakos's idea to start this type of course after World War II. He was able to get certification so that returning soldiers could attend the training under the GI bill. The twentieth candy school was held in July 2000.

That's just one way that Pulakos has demonstrated cutting-edge thinking for almost a century. According to Joy Pulakos, George's mother, Pulakos was the first retail store in Erie to be air-conditioned and the first to serve ice cream year-round. More recently, Pulakos began using insulated, iced shipping containers to solve the problem summer temperatures present for transporting chocolates.

It's interesting to hear George Pulakos's thoughts on the art and science of candy making. "The science is what we teach at the candy school. Without the science, you can't have the art. For example, water and chocolate don't mix. If you get water in the wrong areas, you can get into problems with bacteria. You have to know what you can and can't do. The art is knowing what's going on when you're producing something, knowing how to adjust the process so you maintain consistency day in and day out.

Four generations of Pulakos Chocolates: George P. and Gus Pulakos, in portraits, the late Herk (seated), and current president, George A. Pulakos. COURTESY OF PULAKOS 926 CHOCOLATES

"As with any industry, computers have taken over in processing," he adds. "You could run your entire process remotely from inside an office. We have a lot of modern equipment; however, we still maintain a very hands-on operation." Even with the proliferation of machinery, there's still plenty of room for creativity in chocolate making. New molds and sculptures are being designed all the time. Pulakos has developed chocolate plaques representing some of Erie's landmarks: Presque Isle State Park, the city skyline, and the Flagship *Niagara*. Pulakos personnel had the honor of presenting a plaque shaped like the state of Pennsylvania to Gov. Tom Ridge as part of a Pennsylvania Manufacturing Confectioners Association meeting.

Today, Pulakos 926 Chocolates has about fifty employees, who make and sell a complete line of candy, including fudges, nougats, caramels, and creams. Sponge taffy is a favorite; chocolate-covered fruits and nuts are also popular. For a unique taste of autumn, try the apple chips dipped in milk chocolate, flavored with caramel or cinnamon.

The Tour

"Feel free to ask questions," deadpans George Pulakos. "If I don't know the answer, I'll make something up and you'll never know the difference!"

Pulakos Chocolates moved to this location at 926 State Street, Erie, in 1908. COURTESY OF PULAKOS 926 CHOCOLATES

That sets the tone for a tour that's fun and educational; despite the disclaimer, George knows as much about candy making as anyone in the business. And he should. According to his mother, Joy, George has been making candy since he was six years old.

The tour spends ten to fifteen minutes in the heart of the operation, the kitchen. Flavors and colors line the walls and shelves. George explains the difference between chocolate makers and candy makers. "Very few candy makers actually make their own chocolate from cocoa beans," he says. "There are a few big chocolate manufacturers, and candy makers purchase from them." Using a recipe handed down through four generations, Pulakos blends chocolate from three different sources to achieve its signature taste.

Chocolate arrives as 10-pound blocks packed into 1,700-pound totes. When Pulakos is ready to use the chocolate, it's melted and blended in a 5,000-pound tank, then piped through the factory to where it's needed. "Once it goes into the tank, we don't touch it until

Visiting Pulakos 926 Chocolates

ERIE, PA

Fax number: 814-456-4876

E-mail: e-mail@pulakoschocolates.com

Tour hours: Monday–Friday,
10 A.M.–3 P.M., September–April.
Retail store open Monday–Saturday,
9:30 A.M.–6:30 P.M.

Admission: Free.

Reservations: Required.

Special considerations: Wheelchair
accessible. No age restrictions.
Strollers permitted. No photography
permitted. The tour goes through a
working factory. Wear closed-toed,
nonskid shoes.

Tour length and type: 45-minute
guided tour of the factory floor.

Group size: Maximum of forty to fifty
people per tour. Individuals and
families welcome. Small groups
may be combined.

On-site facilities: Retail store.
No public restrooms.

Nearby attractions: Contact the Erie
Area Convention and Visitors Bureau
at 800-542-ERIE or visit the website
www.eriepa.com for information about
Erie attractions, including the Erie
Art Museum, Erie Historical Museum,
Erie Maritime Museum and U.S. Brig
Niagara, Presque Isle State Park,
Waldameer Park and Water World,
and wineries. Troyer Potato Products,
a potato chip factory in nearby Water-
ford, also welcomes visitors.

Directions: At the intersection of PA
Route 8 and U.S. Route 20.

we achieve the finished products,"
George says.

In the next room is the chocolate
bar line. This is where Pulakos manu-
factures and packages candy bars for
fund-raising organizations. In subsequent rooms, you see the enrobing
lines, where filled candies are coated
with chocolate, as well as molding operations, wrapping, and packing.

"Tourists sometimes ask us if our
chocolate looks so shiny because we
put paraffin wax in it, like housewives
used to in the old days," George says.
"Of course we don't, and neither does
any other manufacturer. It's illegal."
Pulakos chocolates have their beautiful shine because they are tempered
just right. In other words, the mixing
and temperatures have been ideally
managed.

People frequently comment on the
cleanliness of the operation. This is obviously something that Pulakos takes
very seriously. "We shut down a half
hour early every day for cleanup,"
George says. "If you keep up on a daily
basis, cleanup is a lot easier. We also
hire private consultants—food processing experts and some ex-FDA employees—to inspect our plant. This isn't
required, but we think it's important."

The last stop on the tour is the retail store, which sells gift-shop items as
well as candy. Here you finish your tour
with a sample of Pulakos chocolate.

Wilbur Chocolate Candy Americana Museum & Store

48 North Broad Street
Lititz, PA 17543
717-626-3459 or 888-299-5287
www.wilburbuds.com

You may be familiar with the name Wilbur Chocolate because of those delicious little Wilbur Buds, but candy makers and baking companies all over the country know Wilbur as a major supplier of chocolate and other quality ingredients. Wilbur sells more than 150 million pounds of products each year.

The company no longer offers tours of the factory floor. Instead, visitors are welcome to peruse the Candy Americana Museum at the site. There are several rooms of candy-making artifacts and related items, including a working candy kitchen. There's also a video presentation of chocolate making the Wilbur way and a large retail store that sells the company's confections, including the famous Wilbur Buds.

In 1865, as the Civil War was coming to a close, H. O. Wilbur was the proprietor of a hardware and stove business in Vineland, New Jersey. He saw an opportunity and changed careers, joining Samuel Croft in the confectionery business in Philadelphia. The partners started their candy business at 125 North Third Street under the name Croft and Wilbur. With manufacturing equipment that consisted of a kettle, a coal fire, some buckets, and a marble slab, they produced molasses candies and hard candies, which were purchased by the railroad company and sold by train boys.

Business was good, and Croft and Wilbur moved to 1226 Market Street. When that space also proved too small in 1884, the principals decided that a separate factory should make chocolate, rather than other kinds of candy. A new company, H. O. Wilbur and Sons, manufactured the chocolate products. Croft got a new partner and continued the candy business under the name Croft and Allen.

Three years later, H. O. Wilbur needed larger quarters once again. The company moved to another Philadelphia site at Third, New, and Bread Streets. Business was so successful that H. O. Wilbur retired early at age fifty-nine. Two of his three sons, William Nelson Wilbur and

Harry L. Wilbur, took over. When Harry died in 1900, H. O.'s third son, Bertram K., returned from practicing medicine in Alaska to supervise production in the chocolate plant.

In order to improve Wilbur's chocolate-making process, William Nelson Wilbur brought two brothers, Steve and Mass Oriole, from France in the early 1890s. These experienced confectioners helped develop the distinctive rich taste of Wilbur chocolate.

A third-generation Wilbur, Lawrence H., was trained in Germany and tutored by Steve Oriole. We have him to thank for developing the machine that foil-wrapped the famous buds, which were introduced in 1893.

The firm was incorporated as H. O. Wilbur and Sons in January 1909. In 1913, the company needed more room and constructed a third building between two existing ones in Lititz. In 1928, as part of a merger, the company name changed to Wilbur-Suchard Chocolate Company, Inc. Brewster-Ideal Chocolate Co. of Lititz and Newark, New Jersey, was part of this strategic move.

See candy made the old-fashioned way at Wilbur Chocolate Candy Americana Museum & Store.

Together, the three factories produced a complete line of chocolate items for retail sale. By the mid-1930s, the Philadelphia operation had been completely moved to Lititz, and the Newark plant was sold. When the production and sale of Suchard items was discontinued in 1958, the corporate name was changed to Wilbur Chocolate Company. Since 1992, Wilbur Chocolate Company has been part of Cargill, Incorporated, whose main business is trading grains and processing agricultural commodities.

The Candy Americana Museum traces the history of the company and the chocolate manufacturing industry. It's fascinating to see the old metal molds, tins, and boxes as they evolved

Visiting Wilbur Chocolate

LITITZ, PA

Fax number: 717-626-3463

Tour hours: Monday–Saturday, 10 A.M. to 5 P.M. year-round.

Admission: Free.

Reservations: Please call ahead, especially for groups.

Special considerations: Not wheelchair accessible. No age restrictions. Strollers permitted, but they must be carried up five steps to get into the building. Still and video cameras permitted.

Tour length and type: 15 to 30 minutes. Self-guided tour through candy museum; 8-minute video of manufacturing process.

Group size: Maximum of forty-five people. Individuals and families welcome.

On-site facilities: Retail store. Restrooms next door at the visitors center.

Nearby attractions: Contact the Pennsylvania Dutch Convention and Visitors Bureau at 800-PA-DUTCH or visit the website www.padutchcountry.com for information about Lancaster-area attractions, including Dutch Wonderland family amusement park, Ephrata Cloister, factory outlets, James Buchanan's Wheatland, Landis Valley Museum, National Watch and Clock Museum, Railroad Museum of Pennsylvania, Strasburg Railroad Company, wineries, and more. Sturgis Pretzel House and the Cake And Kandy Emporium, both in Lititz, welcome visitors, as do the Intercourse Canning Company and the Intercourse Pretzel Factory, in nearby Intercourse.

In Lititz, the Lititz Historical Foundation offers a brochure outlining a self-guided walking tour. Pick one up at the Johannes Mueller House, 137–139 East Main Street. Lititz Springs Park is a nice spot to relax; the visitors center is at the park's entrance. Kready's Country Store Museum is an original 1860s country store that's open to visitors. Pick up brochures at any attraction.

Directions: From the intersection of U.S. Route 30 and PA Route 772 in Gap, take Route 772 West to Lititz. This becomes East Main Street. It comes to a T at Broad Street (PA Route 501). Turn right. Wilbur Chocolate Candy Americana Museum and Store is on the left almost immediately. Park on the street or turn left into the Lititz Springs Park lot.

Or, from PA Route 501 and U.S. Route 30, take Route 501 North. As soon as you cross Main Street in Lititz, look for Wilbur on your left. Park on the street or turn left into the Lititz Springs Park lot.

over the past century and a half. A short video explains how the cocoa bean is processed into the delicious stuff we know as chocolate. Other fun things on display include your candy horoscope, candy curling machines, and a scale model of a tall ship made entirely of chocolate.

The museum has an interesting collection of chocolate pots from all over the world. There are pieces from prestigious manufacturers like Dresden and Limoges, along with lesser-known but equally interesting specimens. They're just as fascinating from a social history perspective as they are for their fine details.

Chocolate was popular as a drink long before it was eaten as candy. You may consider the English to be inveterate tea drinkers, but in Oliver Cromwell's time—the mid-1600s—chocolate was the fashionable English beverage. Chocolate houses appeared all over London. Drinking chocolate was touted as being wholesome for body and mind, and it was often consumed for medicinal purposes. The famous diarist Samuel Pepys is said to have sipped chocolate first thing in the morning to settle his stomach.

The social aspects of getting together to drink chocolate soon became more important than the health benefits. Because only a small segment of the population could afford the relatively high cost of chocolate drinks, London's chocolate houses began to get a reputation as fashionable gathering spots for male society—the original men's clubs. They were not always bastions of impeccable behavior, however. Gambling, gossip, and political scheming prompted Charles II to briefly ban chocolate houses in 1675.

The chocolate pot—much like the teapot—became the most prominent object for this social custom. Pots were used to make and serve drinking chocolate and were designed to ensure that someone could constantly stir the chocolate to prevent the settling of sediment. Chocolate pots had either hinged or removable covers. More than 150 hand-painted antique porcelain European and Asian chocolate pots are on view in the museum.

The museum was the brainchild of Penny Buzzard, wife of Wilbur's former president, John Buzzard. Back in 1972, Penny Buzzard started looking for chocolate-related items at antique shows and flea markets. Before long, she had gathered more than a thousand items to put on display in the museum. Friends and associates donated early candy machinery, marble slabs, starch trays, copper kettles, and other related items.

In 1977, a working candy kitchen was added to the museum area. You can watch one or more ladies making candy by hand, including marshmallows, almond bark, peanut butter meltaways, and almond butter crunch. Don't forget to pick up your free sample of Wilbur Buds. And if that's not enough, the Candy Americana Store offers every kind of Wilbur confection you could possibly want.

Wolfgang Candy Company

50 East Fifth Avenue
York, PA 17404
717-843-5536 or 800-248-4273
www.wolfgangcandy.com

One look at the half-timbered building surrounded by tidy flowerbeds, and you know right away that Wolfgang Candy Company is true to Old World traditions. Its tasty nickname, Das Sweeten Haus, needs no translation. Come inside to explore a museum-type display, shop for fresh candy, and get a drink at the soda fountain. While you're perched on a counterside stool, watch the video presentation that explains how Wolfgang candy is made. When the film concludes, you'll be well prepared for the highlight of your visit: a tour of the factory to see candy making in action.

The spacious, brick-floored lobby in the headquarters/distribution center building houses a range of historical displays worth a look. The old candy-making equipment and paraphernalia include antique molds and tins, fruit drop rollers, and a crimped-edge butter cutter, which fashioned ravioli-shaped butter slices. A glass-fronted counter contains some of the ingredients Wolfgang uses, such as toasted coconut, sugar, filberts, flour, and cocoa powder. A poster carousel presents old correspondence and receipts, mostly from the 1930s and 1940s. Read the "Woman's Law from Commonwealth of PA Act of 1913," which imposed restrictions on where, when, and how long women could work.

Wolfgang's 1993 Fancy Food Packaging Award for its "dandy candy truck" is also on view, as is the company's 1997 York Courthouse collectible box. The box was produced by the company to commemorate the anniversary of the November 1777 Continental Congress convention in York, at which the Articles of Confederation were adopted. A 1926 Ford Model T is parked in the center of the room. Another eye-catcher is the Schell family dollhouse. Press the button on the wall, and electric lights turn on inside. The fantasy structure, built in 1978 by George Schell for his daughter, is four stories tall and filled with furniture.

The Old World–style entrance to Wolfgang Candy Company, Das Sweeten Haus.

Once you've looked at the displays, browsed the shop, and watched the video, join your group in the lobby to take a firsthand look at Wolfgang's candy-making operations.

The Tour

D. E. Wolfgang started the candy company that bears his name in 1921. His five children and some of their children followed in his footsteps. Wolfgang is still family owned and operated.

The building you're standing in serves as the distribution center. Raw materials are delivered and stored here, then moved to the two factory buildings nearby as needed. Finished products come back to this building. The overwhelming majority of Wolfgang's business—97 percent of it—is for fund-raising. More than two thousand organizations sell Wolfgang to raise funds, and Wolfgang candy is distributed in twenty-six states, west to Michigan, south to North Carolina, and north to Maine.

The candy is made across the street, in former homes that over the years became a factory. Your guide takes you on a short walk to the main factory and up the steps to see the candy kitchen.

This is where butter creams, marshmallows, and other centers are crafted. There's a heated tank on the roof that holds corn syrup and sugar. Wolfgang also buys its milk chocolate in liquid form, storing it in two 45,000-gallon tanks.

You might get the opportunity to see trays of cornstarch being stamped to create temporary molds. After the candy sets in the molds, the candy is released, and the starch is reused. Finished candy is sifted

Visiting Wolfgang Candy Company

YORK, PA

Mailing address: P.O. Box 226, York, PA 17405

Fax number: 717-845-2881

Tour hours: Monday–Friday, 8 A.M.–3 P.M. September–Easter. The rest of the year, one tour is given daily, Monday–Friday, at 10:00 A.M. Candy shop open Monday–Friday, 8 A.M.–5 P.M.; Saturdays, 9 A.M.–4 P.M.

Reservations: Large groups must call at least one week in advance.

Special considerations: Retail store is wheelchair accessible; factory is not. No age restrictions. Strollers permitted in the retail store but not in the factory. Still and video cameras permitted. The tour goes through a working factory. Wear closed-toed, nonskid shoes. Be prepared to walk about two blocks total, and to go up and down steps. It can get loud in parts of the factory, so you may want to take along earplugs.

Tour length and type: 45 minutes to 1 hour. Half-hour video presentation in retail shop, followed by guided tour of the factory buildings.

Group size: Maximum of twenty people per tour. Individuals and families welcome.

On-site facilities: Candy shop, soda fountain, ice cream, restrooms, museum-type displays.

Nearby attractions: Contact the York County Convention and Visitors Bureau at 888-858-YORK or visit the website www.yorkpa.org for information about attractions, including the Agricultural Museum of York County, Harley-Davidson Motorcycle Final Assembly Plant and Museum, the Historical Society Museum/York County Heritage Trust, and the York Barbell Museum and Weightlifting Hall of Fame. Martin's Potato Chips in York, Snyder's of Hanover, and Utz Quality Foods in Hanover also welcome visitors.

Directions: From U.S. Route 30 in York, go south on North George Street. Turn left onto East Fourth Avenue (approximately eight blocks). Wolfgang Candy Company is on the right.

and brushed to remove any remaining starch, then is sent through a trapdoor to the floor below.

Downstairs is the enrobing area. It might feel a bit warm, since an ambient temperature of 88 degrees is optimal for coating. Watch nuts or other centers get coated bottom, then top, as they move down the line on conveyor belts. The cooling tunnel sets the chocolate so that the candies release easily from the belt.

Now the tour heads outside again, for a brief walk down the block to another factory building, where hollow chocolates and clusters are made. Follow your guide down the steps to the basement, and you'll see some unique machinery used for making hollow items.

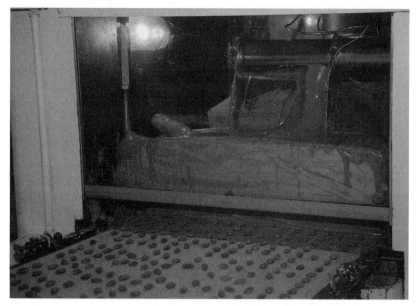

Candy centers are coated with chocolate, then cooled in a special tunnel.

After chocolate is dispensed into a mold, the mold is placed in a metal frame. Each frame weighs about 30 pounds. A few dozen frames are attached by magnets to the outside of a large cylinder, until it looks like a cross between an MRI scanner and a porcupine, then the entire assembly is spun around. Centrifugal force pushes the chocolate to the outside of the molds evenly, resulting in perfect hollow chocolates. After the frames are unclipped, the molds are moved into a cold tunnel, where they chill at 55 degrees. Finished hollow chocolates are popped out, ready for packaging.

After a stop near the cluster-making area, you return to the distribution area. This time, you enter the building through the impressive warehouse, where orders are picked from a rack system. Although Wolfgang's candy-making methods are traditional, the company's inventory management is twenty-first-century state-of-the-art. Integrated distribution and accounting systems track orders from the time they're taken until they're delivered.

Your tour concludes where it began, with a sample or two of fresh chocolate in the shop.

REGIONAL SPECIALTIES

A s you travel through Pennsylvania, you'll have the opportunity to sample snacks and other foods that have a strong regional association, such as cheese steaks in Philadelphia or shoo-fly pie in Lancaster County. Farm stands on backroads all over the state offer homegrown produce, home-baked goods, and hometown hospitality.

It's worthwhile to visit two establishments where the foods are pure Pennsylvania. Intercourse Canning Company's products are a tribute to the bounty of the Amish garden, preserved in relishes and condiments. Seltzer's Smokehouse Meats is known for its Lebanon bologna, developed here almost a century ago.

Intercourse Canning Company

3612 East Newport Road
Intercourse, PA 17534
717-768-0156
www.intercoursecanning.com

There's something so appealing about the sight of neatly stacked glass jars filled with fruits and vegetables. Maybe it's the tidy way things are lined up. Perhaps it's the jewel-tone colors. Or it could be a bit of nostalgia for homemade foods that someone special once prepared for us.

Whatever the reason, you can get that wonderful feeling at Intercourse Canning Company, where proprietor Susan Adams and her staff prepare, display, and sell foods they refer to as Amish hors d'oeuvres. There's no official tour, but guests are invited to watch the canning process in the glass-enclosed kitchen. Lots of samples are available throughout the store, prettily displayed in clear bowls with crackers or chips to spread them on. Gentle music adds just the right touch to the atmosphere.

Nestled in the heart of Pennsylvania Dutch Country, the FDA-certified Intercourse Canning Company is 3,000 square feet of tempting pickles, vegetables, relishes, salads, salsas, jams, and jellies freshly canned by local Amish and Mennonite folk. The most asked-about item? "Probably chow-chow," says Adams. "People who aren't from the area might not be familiar with it. Chow-chow is really an end-of-garden salad. Typically, our Amish neighbors use whatever is left over in the garden, so it's not the same every time. Ours is a very precise recipe of vegetables."

The large space is arranged with wide aisles, so there's plenty of room to accommodate motor coach tours and other large gatherings easily. Groups have visited from all over the United States, as well as abroad. They're treated to a five- to ten-minute talk that describes what's going on in the cannery on the other side of the windows. "Giving group tours is the most fun," says Adams, with a smile. "This year we had people from Paris, from Canada, from Japan, from Australia. They tour the United States and spend several days visiting here in Lancaster County."

Believe it or not, we have Emperor Napoleon I to thank for the canning method of food preservation. The French Army was plagued by malnutrition in the late eighteenth century, and Napoleon needed a way to feed his growing military forces. At his behest, the executive branch of the French government sponsored a contest, offering 12,000 francs to anyone who could invent a way to preserve food for the troops.

Nicolas Appert, Parisian chef, candy maker, and amateur scientist, the self-educated son of an innkeeper, knew how to pickle food and brew beer. He also noticed that wine did not spoil when it was kept in airtight bottles. Appert filled glass bottles with food, corked them, heated them in boiling water, then sealed them tightly with pitch, thereby preventing the food from spoiling. By 1804, Appert had opened a vacuum-packing plant. The French Navy used his principles to preserve meat, fruits, vegetables, and milk. Appert received his prize money in 1810. He published his findings and in 1812 was awarded a gold medal by the Society for the Encouragement of National Industry.

The method quickly made its way across the English Channel, and in 1810, Englishman Peter Durand patented the use of airtight tin-plated wrought-iron containers for food preservation. Although the process has

Gleaming jars fill the shelves at Intercourse Canning Company.

been refined over the years, the basic principles have remained intact for two centuries.

Canning is one of the best ways to preserve food. Heating destroys microorganisms, and since canned food is thoroughly cooked, no additives are needed to preserve the foods. Fruits and vegetables can be canned at their peak, when they look and taste their best. They're also high in nutrients, since the time between harvest and processing is minimal.

Intercourse Canning Company encourages visitors to taste the results; many products are available each day for sampling. The staff is very friendly, always willing to answer questions. "We encourage people to browse through the cannery. They're welcome to take pictures, even of the actual canning operation," says Adams. "Also, I think children do not understand how food is processed," she adds. "Lots of children think that milk comes from the grocery store, when milk really comes from a cow. There's a lot of education they can get by watching the canning process."

Visiting Intercourse Canning Company

INTERCOURSE, PA

Mailing address: P.O. Box 541, Intercourse, PA 17534.

Fax number: 717-768-0158

E-mail address: info@intercoursecanning.com

Tour hours: January–April, canning takes place Monday–Friday, 10 A.M.–3:30 P.M., and store hours are Monday–Saturday, 10 A.M.–4 P.M. May–December, canning takes place Monday–Friday, 9:30 A.M.–4:30 P.M., and store hours are Monday–Saturday, 9:30 A.M.–5 P.M.

Admission: Free. Special sampling for groups is available for $3 per person.

Reservations: Requested for groups.

Special considerations: Wheelchair accessible, including restrooms. No age restrictions. Strollers permitted. Still and video cameras permitted.

Tour length and type: Groups get a short talk from a staff member; individuals and families watch the process as a self-guided tour. You can watch the canning process for as long as you like. Allow about 10 minutes to observe, plus at least 15 minutes to shop.

Group size: Maximum of a busload of people per tour. Individuals and families welcome.

On-site facilities: Retail store, restrooms, front porch sitting area.

Special events: Anniversary sale in July.

Nearby attractions: Contact the Pennsylvania Dutch Convention and Visitors Bureau at 800-PA-DUTCH or visit the website www.padutchcountry.com for information about Lancaster-area attractions, including Dutch Wonderland family amusement park, Ephrata Cloister, factory outlets, James Buchanan's Wheatland, Landis Valley Museum, National Watch and Clock Museum, Railroad Museum of Pennsylvania, Strasburg Railroad Company, wineries, and more. Intercourse Pretzel Factory is in the small shopping center across the street. Anderson Bakery Company (Anderson Pretzels) in Lancaster also welcomes visitors, as do several sites in Lititz: the Cake And Kandy Emporium, Sturgis Pretzel House, and Wilbur Chocolate Candy Americana Museum & Store.

Directions: From U.S. Route 30, take PA Route 772 West. Intercourse Canning Company is adjacent to the Best Western Motor Inn on left side of Route 772E just southeast of PA Route 340.

Besides the chow-chow, some of the other Amish country treats include pickled sweet baby beets, marinated mushrooms, and Grammy Betty's banana pickles. Several hundred products are offered in all; ask a staff member for a list so you can mail in an order later on. Intercourse Canning Company also sells gourmet coffee—including a snickerdoodle-flavored blend—pancake mixes, handmade soaps, and lotions, plus T-shirts and sweatshirts for anyone who wants a more lasting reminder of the visit.

Seltzer's Smokehouse Meats

230 North College Street
Palmyra, PA 17078
717-838-6336 or 800-282-6336
www.seltzerslebanonbologna.com

Seltzer's Smokehouse Meats no longer gives plant tours. However, if you like bologna and you're in the area, by all means pay a visit to the outlet store in Palmyra and watch the seven-minute video. You'll learn a lot about the company and its products, and you'll be offered plenty of tasty samples. Take along a sweatshirt, because the counter area is almost as cold as a meat locker.

Seltzer's is the largest single producer of Lebanon bologna in the United States. Over the past century, the company has developed a niche market for its high-quality, lean smoked meat products. Two items dominate the line: regular and sweet Lebanon bologna.

The man who originated these recipes was butcher Harvey Seltzer, who in 1902, developed a unique, savory blend of beef and spices. Seltzer was following in the footsteps of the resourceful Pennsylvania Germans, who had incorporated Old World butchering, curing, and sausage-making skills into their Lebanon County farm lives. The bologna was so popular that Seltzer went commercial with it.

The original recipe has been passed down in the family. Harvey Seltzer's descendants continue to provide the taste for which Seltzer's brand meats became famous. Seltzer's Smokehouse Meats also maintains its dedication to the quality, service, and integrity that are Pennsylvania Dutch essentials. Along with products, the company offers marketing and other support to its distributors and retailers.

Video Tour

Each week, Seltzer's takes 60 tons of 90 percent lean, boneless meat. The meat is coarsely ground and blended with salt, sugar, spices, and potassium nitrate. Four hundred tubs a day are transported to the Palmyra plant.

The chunks are broken apart, then finely ground. The meat is passed through a metal detector, then goes through an automatic stuffer to be

Visiting Seltzer's

PALMYRA, PA

Mailing address: P.O. Box 111, Palmyra, PA 17078.

Fax number: 717-838-5345

E-mail address: seltzerssmokehouse meats@worldnet.att.net

Tour hours: Monday–Friday, 7 A.M.–5 P.M.; Saturday, 7 A.M.–11 A.M. Open year-round, except holidays.

Admission: Free.

Reservations: Groups must call in advance; reservations unnecessary for individuals or families.

Special considerations: Wheelchair accessible. No age restrictions. Strollers permitted. Still and video cameras permitted, but there's not much to take pictures of. Take along a sweatshirt, as the counter area is cold.

Tour length and type: 7-minute video tour.

Group size: Maximum of about fifteen people can fit comfortably in the counter area. Individuals and families welcome.

On-site facilities: Factory outlet store. No public restrooms.

Nearby attractions: Contact the Harrisburg–Hershey–Carlisle–Perry County Tourism and Convention Bureau at 800-995-0969 or visit the website www.visithhc.com for information on attractions, including Cornwall Iron Furnace, Hershey Gardens, Hershey Museum, HersheyPark, Indian Echo Caverns, the State Capitol, and the State Museum of Pennsylvania. Hershey's Chocolate World also welcomes visitors for a simulated factory tour.

Directions: Located at 230 North College Street, just three blocks north of U.S. Route 422 in Palmyra, 3 miles east of Hershey.

packed into casings. Next, the bologna goes into a smokehouse that's designed the same way Harvey Seltzer's was in 1902. The firepit contains hardwoods like oak and hickory. Sawdust on the smokehouse floor is sprinkled with water, creating just the right amount of smoke. Protective stockinettes on the meats let the smoke penetrate the casing while the moisture escapes.

After three days smoking at a temperature of around 100 degrees, the meat is cured. About 20 to 25 percent of the bolognas are sliced and packaged in 6-ounce to 1-pound packages. The rest of the meats are halved and vacuum-sealed before being sent to delis. In addition to putting its own name on products, Seltzer's also packs meat for private labels, including A&P, Hatfield Meats, Kessler's, and Kroger. An inspection stamp bearing the number 474 indicates a Seltzer's product, no matter what the label says.

The company prides itself not only on the flavor of its meats, but also on the quality and safety of its products. The meat is lean or 95 percent fat-free beef, with no water or fillers. When the federal government started inspecting meat-packing plants, Seltzer's was the first federally inspected Lebanon bologna company, and it's one of the oldest continually USDA-inspected operations in the country.

Seltzer's Smokehouse Meats is famous for its Lebanon bologna.

When the video presentation ends, help yourself to some of the bologna, beef sticks, and other samples on the table behind you. You'll understand what makes Seltzer's products so special.

Acknowledgments

My first thank-you goes to a company that doesn't even exist anymore: the Bond Bakery in Philadelphia. When I was four years old, I took my first factory tour there. I can still remember the wonderful smells, the whirring machinery, the way the loaves of bread were shot into plastic bags, and the free loaf of delicious, fresh coffee-cake bread that I got to take home with me. Many of you have similar fond memories of factory tours. There's something wonderful about watching products—especially food products—made right before your eyes.

I owe a debt of gratitude to personnel at tourism promotion agencies, convention and visitors bureaus, and chambers of commerce throughout Pennsylvania. Their help was invaluable in identifying likely candidates for inclusion in *Pennsylvania Snacks*.

This book would not have been possible without the time and energy expended by staff members at all of the sites covered. These good people returned my calls, answered my e-mails, filled out questionnaires, took me on tours, reviewed preliminary versions of the text for accuracy, and in some cases provided photographs. One of the nicest parts of this project was getting to meet many of those folks face-to-face.

The following people were particularly helpful to me: Linda R. Yost of Anderson Bakery Co., Inc.; Denise Bruno and Emma Hodgson of Asher's Chocolates; Jack Asher and Judith Folk of Asher's/Lewistown; Nancy Fasolt of the Cake And Kandy Emporium; Jean Daffin, Stan Lefes, Connie Leon, and Gary Sigler of Daffin's Candies; David Golembeski of Sherm Edwards Candies; Suzanne Egan of Egan Advertising; Kristin Barrett of Gardners Candies; Cindy Staub at graphics plus; Jennifer Arrigo of Herr Foods, Inc.; Todd A. Kohr of Hershey's Chocolate World; Susan J. Adams of Intercourse Canning Company; Donna Clark of Intercourse Pretzel Factory; Tonja McCauley and Kenneth A. Potter Jr. of Martin's Potato Chips, Inc.; Georgia Macris and Carol Murdoch of Philadelphia Candies; Steve Porter of Porter Design; Sheila Linhart, George A. Pulakos, and Joy Pulakos of Pulakos 926 Chocolates; Agnes Bender and David Reeber of Seltzer's Smokehouse Meats; Christopher Long of Snyder's of Hanover; Michael Tshudy of Sturgis Pretzel House; Linda L. Kane of Troyer Potato

Products, Inc.; Pamela Berwager, Gary Laabs, and Michael Rice of Utz Quality Foods, Inc.; Michelle Griffith and Barbara Jo Metzler of Wilbur Chocolate Candy Americana Museum & Store; and Robert L. Wolfgang of Wolfgang Candy.

Kyle Weaver, my editor at Stackpole Books, deserves the credit for coming up with the concept for this book. He and assistant editor Amy Cooper shepherded me through the writing and production process with kindness and expertise.

I dedicate this book to Howard Shapiro, editor *extraordinaire,* who has no idea how much he changed my life by giving me that first assignment.

There is no way I could have accepted the obligation to take on this project, let alone fulfilled that obligation, without the support of my family and friends. My parents, Babe and Seymour Hernes, and my sister, Helene Silverman, are unflagging cheerleaders for my writing career. Jason and Steven, my children, are the most enthusiastic young helpers and fun traveling companions I could ever hope for. My deepest gratitude goes to my husband, Alan B. Silverman, my fellow traveler to snack factories and in life.

Index

Page numbers in *italics* indicate illustrations and sidebars.